SO-AIL-779

THE WORLD-WIDE INDUSTRIAL ENTERPRISE

McKINSEY FOUNDATION LECTURE SERIES

Sponsored by the
Graduate School of Business, Columbia University

THE WORLD-WIDE
INDUSTRIAL
ENTERPRISE

ITS CHALLENGE AND PROMISE

FREDERIC G. DONNER
Chairman, General Motors Corporation

McGraw-Hill Book Company

NEW YORK   TORONTO   LONDON   SYDNEY

THE WORLD-WIDE INDUSTRIAL ENTERPRISE

Copyright © 1967 by the Trustees of Columbia University in the City of New York. All Rights Reserved. Printed in the United States of America. This book, or parts thereof, may not be reproduced in any form without permission of the publishers. *Library of Congress Catalog Card Number 66-28632*

17601

1234567890VB72106987

PREFACE

An experience of profound significance is found in this account of the overseas expansion of the General Motors Corporation. As the leader in the world-wide automobile industry, the company has been a major participant in the development of the pattern of economic progress around the globe. During a period when many governments have sought through trade and aid to stimulate world development, perhaps no single influence has directly or indirectly contributed more to the material well-being of the world.

While development programs generally have often focused on the transfer of capital, hopefully accompanied by the transfer of skills and methods, the emphasis in the General Motors experience has been just the reverse. It took a commitment of capital to get started, but increments to the initial investment generally have been self-generated or locally financed rather than provided through additional funds from the parent company. What have been continuously transferred in very large quantities are the policies, practices, and skills that have been so successfully applied in the parent organization, modified of course, to adapt to local situations.

The General Motors record of overseas expansion in the postwar years is dramatic. From a commitment of about $180 million of net working capital and fixed assets in 1950, the figure has grown, almost entirely from funds self-generated and from local borrowings, to approximately $1.1 billion. That is about six times as much capital as was committed a decade and a half ago. The ability to produce and distribute motor vehicles during the same period has correspondingly expanded; from 180,000 cars and trucks in 1950 to 1,200,000 in 1965. The 155,000 overseas employees are of many nationalities, less than 300 being assigned from the home office. What an impact on the world's material well-being, and accomplished primarily through the transfer of skills rather than capital!

Perhaps the most significant yet least appreciated and understood characteristic of many postwar development programs is that the provision of capital can get ahead of the capacity to use capital effectively; this probably has happened in many of the postwar development programs. On the other hand, the construction of an organization with technical and administrative skills to maximize the effectiveness of investment seldom is accompanied by a sustained shortage of capital, even in capital-short regions of the world. The corporation, as an organization, provides the framework for the communication of administrative skills and technology. These lectures demonstrate vividly the contribution of one of the world's most important multi-national corporations, not only in furnishing managerial and technical skills, know-how, employment, training and new products, but also in stimulating a variety of complementary industries.

Mr. Frederic G. Donner, Board Chairman and Chief Executive Officer of the General Motors Corporation, in presenting the eleventh series of the Columbia-McKinsey Lectures, is mainly interested in recalling how the policies and practices of the parent organization have been adapted and applied to its rapidly growing activities in foreign countries—particularly in West Germany, England, Australia and several South American countries. The company now operates motor vehicle manufacturing plants in seven countries (outside of the United States and Canada) and assembles automobiles in seven additional countries.

The administrative principle of decentralized operating responsibility with coordinated policy control, worked out successfully for domestic operations many years ago, has proved to be equally effective in the global spread of the Corporation's activities. It has permitted overseas subsidiaries to be as fully integrated in the overall company operations as a division or plant in the United States. At the same time, it has facilitated adaptation to the local methods of conducting business and to the social and cultural conditions of different countries.

Mr. Donner is aware of the legitimate desires of many foreign nationals to participate in the profits of corporations made within their borders. In response, Mr. Donner does not recommend "joint ventures" between foreign nationals or foreign governments and subsidiaries of parent corporations in the case of integrated enterprises. The profitability of the overseas subsidiaries of General Motors, he maintains, depends on the "close integration of the subsidiary with the business as a whole." Unified coordination is essential and it would be difficult if not impossible with joint ventures.

As an alternative, Mr. Donner proposes that people of every nationality should have an opportunity to participate in the ownership of the parent company, General Motors. World-wide ownership of the parent would, he urges, retain the advantages of unified co-

ordination of multi-national operations so essential to
efficient operations and profit-making, and at the same
time provide people of other nationalities with the
opportunity to participate in those same profits. Thus,
Mr. Donner wants the stockholders as well as the operations and personnel of General Motors to be multi-
national. He has used imagination in seeking means of
giving foreign citizens the possibility of participating
in the profits of the business.

The experience of General Motors in its overseas
business has, with appropriate variations, been dupli-
cated many times by business corporations of many
nations. The resulting global pattern of mutual interests and associations cuts across national boundaries
and constitutes an interwoven network for the transfer of knowledge, administrative skill and technical
competence that cannot fail to be progressively more
meaningful in man's search for a better way of life.
This global network will also facilitate the transfer
of capital in amounts that are needed to regions
where it can be effectively used.

> COURTNEY C. BROWN
> *Dean, Graduate School of Business*
> *Columbia University*

FOREWORD

This volume represents an expansion of the three Columbia-McKinsey Foundation Lectures which I delivered at Columbia University in the spring of 1966. In preparation of the lectures and the book, I received the benefit of valuable comment and discussion from a number of past and present associates and from several friends outside General Motors. Their suggestions have been of great value in the development of my thesis, and have given greater clarity of expression to the ideas set forth. I would like to acknowledge the many contributions of these individuals and to express my deep appreciation for their assistance and for the competent efforts of the sponsors of the Columbia-McKinsey Lecture Series.

FREDERIC G. DONNER

CONTENTS

1

INTRODUCTION

In the twenty years since the end of the Second World War, the world-wide industrial enterprise has emerged as an important economic institution. Its beginnings trace back well into the last century. During most of the period prior to the Second World War its development was slow, but the seeds had been planted and, in the more favorable economic climates of the postwar years, growth has been vigorous.

It is more than coincidence that this period of rapid growth of world-wide industrial business has been one in which industrial development was a primary and continuing goal of sovereign nations throughout the world. In the advanced countries of North America and Western Europe, and in Japan and Australia, industrial and economic progress has been spectacular by any standard. In many developing countries the growth of basic industries and the expanding use of transportation are now well under way.

World-wide industrial enterprise has played an important role in this postwar economic advance. It has contributed to the growth of industry wherever market potentials held promise and national policies were compatible with private enterprise. A new chapter has opened in the history of world trade and investment

—one that is vigorous, growth conscious and keenly competitive; one that involves firm and lasting commitments in the form of substantial long-term investments in national economies; and one that is consistent with freedom of trade and investment among nations.

The concept of the "world-wide industrial enterprise" that has taken shape includes a number of elements. It is a publicly owned business which may have its headquarters in any nation of the world. It is characterized by a multi-national ownership and a multi-national employee force. It conducts manufacturing and marketing operations in a number of countries, and it exports both from its home base and from subsidiary plants abroad.

In this discussion of the challenge and promise of world-wide enterprise, I draw heavily on my forty years of experience with General Motors. The advantage of this approach which concentrates on a familiar area outweighs, from my point of view, the countermerits of choosing a wider field of business activities and relationships with which I would be less familiar. I have no illusions that the approach of General Motors, or my own business experience, furnishes a pattern which is best for other industrial corporations serving world markets. There may be certain similarities, but every business challenge is in some way unique.

My emphasis is upon the motor vehicle producing and distributing activities of General Motors in countries outside the United States and Canada, excluding the Russian and Chinese spheres of influence with which there has been little or no trade in motor vehicles. The Canadian subsidiaries of General Motors traditionally have not been considered as part of our overseas operations.

2

THE GROWTH OF THE BUSINESS
AND THE DEVELOPMENT
OF AN OPERATING POLICY

THE BASIS FOR A WORLD-WIDE OPERATION
IN THE MOTOR VEHICLE INDUSTRY

A number of factors have combined to influence the growth and development of world-wide motor vehicle operations. First, the types of cars customers want and can afford to buy vary over a wide range from one part of the world to another. In order to serve this variety of demands efficiently, many motor vehicle producers in Europe and North America have established manufacturing facilities to meet the specific product requirements of national markets where volume and profit prospects are promising. In areas of more limited demand, assembly plants have been built to reduce rail and ocean transportation costs and, in many countries, to qualify for a lower rate of import duties on automotive components as compared with fully assembled cars and trucks.

These plants assemble cars and trucks from components shipped to them from one or more manufacturing locations. The flexibility provided by a world network of vehicle manufacturing and assembly facilities makes it possible to supply, with a maximum of efficiency, a distinctive and highly varied product mix suited to each market. Take the specific case of GM

Continental, our assembly plant in Antwerp, Belgium. In 1966, no less than 86 different General Motors makes, models and body styles of both passenger cars and commercial vehicles from General Motors plants in the United States, Canada, England and Germany were scheduled to be assembled under one roof.

There is also the matter of sales and service. Motor vehicles, in common with other complex engineering products, require service and the availability of replacement parts. Since cars and trucks are mobile, service must be reasonably accessible over wide areas. A world-wide business can provide this service because it can support an extensive dealer organization equipped with a wide range of products and parts. The establishment of a strong, aggressive and well-financed dealer network is one of the most important elements in the continuing growth of General Motors world-wide. Every forward step in our progress has confirmed this.

Meeting the expanding world demands for motor vehicles has provided both challenge and opportunity for General Motors over most of the past half century. Over this period, its growth has been evolutionary—influenced by the logistics of world distribution, national policies and the technical nature of the motor vehicle itself.

10

EARLY DEVELOPMENT OF GENERAL
MOTORS OVERSEAS

Prior to the formation of General Motors in 1908, some of the companies that were to make up the enterprise were already participating in overseas markets. The record shows that Oldsmobile and Cadillac were actively engaged in exporting vehicles through dealers and direct sales representatives shortly after the turn of the century. In 1911, less than three years after General Motors was organized, the General Motors Export Company was established to provide, on a systematic and coordinated basis, an overseas distribution framework for the individual car manufacturing operations. The initial capitalization of the Export Company was $10,000 and its sales volume for the six months it operated in 1911 consisted of 100 Buick motor cars.

General Motors began competing in markets overseas by exporting fully assembled vehicles from the United States. Between 1911 and 1922, almost all of its overseas sales were made in this way. Volume was modest by almost any standard. The largest number of fully assembled cars and trucks that were exported by General Motors in this period was about 30,000 in 1920—with about 45 per cent of this total going to Western European markets.

It is fair to say that before 1920 the economic foundations for a world-wide motor vehicle manufacturing enterprise did not exist. The only significant automobile production outside the United States and Canada was in Europe. Individual overseas markets were served partly by exports from this country and Canada, and partly by small producers based mainly in England, France, Germany and Italy. Prior to 1920, the peak reported production of motor vehicles outside North America was about 106,000 units, recorded in 1913, just before the First World War.

Overseas producers generally built cars on a low volume basis at relatively high unit costs. It was thus possible for manufacturers in the United States, with a larger home market and the beginnings of mass production techniques, to be competitive by exporting fully assembled vehicles. Relatively low tariffs on motor vehicles in these early years contributed to the expansion of an export market. Hence, General Motors strategic plans were directed principally toward the development of a distribution network abroad.

STRATEGY OF THE TWENTIES

After 1920, General Motors began to evaluate the advantages of assembling cars overseas from components manufactured in the United States. Several factors made this attractive. With rising incomes in Europe, motor vehicle demand increased rapidly. In

1921, the low point of the twenties, overseas market demand for motor vehicles was slightly more than a quarter of a million units. By 1929, demand had risen to a peak level of about 1.4 million vehicles.

Concurrent with the growth in motor vehicle demand in the twenties, tariffs and other restrictions imposed by several important European countries were reaching levels that made it increasingly difficult for producers in the United States to export fully assembled cars and trucks on a competitive basis. Import duties on fully assembled vehicles were generally higher than those on motor vehicle parts and components. Moreover, transportation economies could be achieved by shipping parts and components for local assembly. For example, in 1928, General Motors could ship nine disassembled Chevrolets to Europe for assembly at about the same shipping cost as two fully assembled cars.

The establishment of assembly facilities in the larger markets of the world promised improvement in General Motors distribution and service system, and ultimately larger sales volumes. As volumes increased, additional dealer sales and service outlets could be franchised. Retail financing and other marketing methods, which had proved their effectiveness in the United States, could also be introduced.

Furthermore, assembly abroad gave General Motors

the opportunity to tailor certain features of its cars—
such as interior styling, color, trim and some acces-
sories—to conform with local tastes. The company
moved in this direction as quickly as local supplying
industries overseas were able to provide quality components and trim on a competitive cost basis.

Assembly of cars overseas required a smaller investment of money and management resources than
would have been necessary for fully integrated manufacturing facilities. Moreover, in the twenties, vehicles
designed for the United States market were still basi-
cally of the same size and type as those produced
abroad. On the cost side, a large market at home en-
abled General Motors to manufacture parts and components and to ship them overseas for assembly into
vehicles which could be priced competitively. Finally,
the assembly of cars overseas permitted more effective
competition with other vehicle manufacturers who
had already adopted or were considering this competitive strategy.

In response to these market forces, General Motors
assembly facilities overseas evolved very naturally out
of its early export business. Field offices, which had
been a necessary part of the export activity, were
steadily enlarged as the business expanded. Seasoned
management, in very short supply during this period,
and technical service employees were added to initial

sales staffs as more functions came to be performed by these distribution centers.

General Motors opened nineteen assembly facilities in fifteen overseas countries between 1923 and 1928. These assembly plants, which were established at strategic locations for competing in world markets, proved to be extremely important in maintaining export volumes from the United States and Canada. By 1929, over 70 per cent of the General Motors cars and trucks exported from North America were shipped as parts and components for assembly overseas.

The decision to establish these assembly facilities in the nineteen twenties was the first of three significant landmarks in General Motors overseas strategy. It laid a foundation for growth. With these facilities, General Motors established firm competitive positions, and made long-term commitments to participate in the emerging world markets for motor vehicles. Valuable experience was gained in operating within varied economic, political and social environments—often markedly different from those of the United States. Not the least important, these years furnished an opportunity to evaluate the basic operating structure and organizational philosophy of General Motors on a world-wide basis.

The intention of General Motors to become an integral part of these overseas markets—together with the expectation of growth in automobile demand that would provide the foundation for expansion overseas —was clearly summarized in our 1924 Annual Report:

> The Corporation's policy in the development of overseas business is to build in the most substantial manner possible, making itself a real factor in the industrial life of each country. A large expansion of overseas business is assured as the economic advantage of the motor car becomes more generally recognized and improved roads are developed.

The experience acquired in operating assembly facilities overseas made it possible to consider a second, and much larger, step forward—the manufacture of cars and trucks overseas. This second step was closely related to the first, and both occurred in the nineteen twenties. Although a major expansion by us in manufacturing overseas did not take place until after the end of the Second World War, a start was made in the second half of the twenties and, in spite of difficulties, real progress was made during the thirties.

Consideration of the strategy of investment in manufacturing facilities abroad was prompted by a number of factors. Incomes overseas were beginning to rise to a level which permitted a small but growing portion of the population to consider the purchase of a car. However, because their incomes were still low relative to those in the United States, an increasing number of potential overseas customers began to call for cars of small size and horsepower. This trend, particularly in Europe, was reinforced by high vehicle operating costs, short distances to be traveled, and local tax systems which discriminated against larger cars, such as those being designed and built in the United States.

With the growth in demand overseas, local producers could and did tailor their cars to their own expanding markets. As their output increased, they became more efficient. Their unit costs were reduced, and they became more competitive in relation to United States producers. Tariffs and restrictions favoring domestic production, such as the so-called McKenna duties in Great Britain, provided these overseas producers with a further advantage.

These factors became increasingly evident as the nineteen twenties progressed. While General Motors was able to make progress overseas on an export and assembly basis during this period, it became clear that the company's competitive position would be further strengthened by the establishment of manufacturing facilities at strategic locations. Thus, in the last half of the twenties, General Motors passed a second major landmark with the purchase of two motor vehicle

17

manufacturing concerns—one in England and one in Germany—to serve as bases for its manufacturing expansion in Europe.

Two major considerations favored the acquisition of established manufacturing companies, rather than the construction of completely new facilities. First, General Motors was convinced that the most important contribution it could make overseas would be in the area of vehicle design and manufacture on a mass production basis. To compete effectively in the shortest possible time, the company would need a product with an accepted name and a strong marketing organization. Second, with a burgeoning market in the United States, seasoned automotive engineers and management personnel were very scarce. At the time, it was not practical for General Motors to consider the large investment of management skill and engineering talent which completely new ventures overseas would require.

Two early efforts to acquire the Citroën facilities in France and the Austin Motor plant in England were unsuccessful. Negotiations with Citroën were terminated in 1919, and discussions with Austin ended in September 1925. Shortly thereafter, near the end of 1925, an agreement was reached to purchase Vauxhall Motors in England. Vauxhall was an old but small producer of relatively high-priced cars with an annual production volume that in 1925 fell short of 1,500 passenger cars. The acquisition of so small a company was recognized as furnishing less than an ideal base for General Motors, but it did provide the opportunity to acquire experience in manufacturing automobiles overseas.

In 1929, General Motors acquired a second overseas manufacturing facility, Adam Opel, which was the largest motor vehicle plant in Germany at the time. In 1928, it had produced nearly 43,000 vehicles, about 30 per cent of the cars and trucks produced in Germany. This company fitted the General Motors concept better than the smaller Vauxhall operation. Opel had a modern, efficient plant and an effective dealer organization. Although it had not developed significant export markets, Opel provided a real basis for growth through the use of the General Motors network of assembly facilities which already had been established overseas.

The operating objectives, which guided General Motors expansion in the twenties and have continued to give direction to its overseas business, were described in the following statement from our 1929 Annual Report:

> The policy which the Corporation is following in the development of its overseas business . . . consists of making General Motors a local institution in each

country in which it is operating, rather than a foreign concern doing business in that country. This is accomplished by recognizing the customs of the country, and harmonizing the Corporation's procedures and policies with such customs. So far as possible, native personnel is employed. The Corporation's products are adapted in the fullest possible measure to the local taste. Experience has shown that in that way the most effective result can be obtained. . . .

The emergence and growth of our overseas manufacturing and assembly operations during the decade of the twenties was accompanied by an equally important expansion and improvement in the efficiency of the overseas distribution and service system. This included further application of the concept of the interchangeability of parts and components which made inventory control easier. Wholesale distributors, who had handled the distribution of General Motors products to retail dealers, were replaced in the larger markets by a growing number of directly franchised local dealers who sold and serviced General Motors products. During this period, General Motors also assumed the responsibility for financing inventories all the way to the point of delivery to the retail dealers. However, in areas where there were no manufacturing or assembly facilities, wholesale distributors continued to play an important function.

During this same decade, the services of the General Motors Acceptance Corporation were extended overseas. This subsidiary had been established in the United States in 1919 to assure that adequate and reliable financing would be available for General Motors dealers and their customers at reasonable cost. From the opening of the first GMAC overseas office in England in 1920 up to the present time, such credit has been provided in many overseas areas. While there are many other overseas sources of financing motor vehicle purchases today, this was not the case when General Motors started. At that time, GMAC's facilities were truly a marketing innovation.

THE THIRTIES: A HOLDING OPERATION

For some time after the important step had been taken with the acquisition of the Vauxhall and Opel plants, General Motors did not expect that its overseas business would depend entirely, or even mainly, on manufacturing overseas. In 1930, for example, when General Motors supplied about one-sixth of the overseas world market demand for motor vehicles, only one in every five of its vehicles sold abroad came from its two overseas manufacturing plants.

It was the influence of the world depression in the early thirties that further intensified the need for manufacturing facilities overseas. The trends in automobile designs in the volume markets overseas and in the United States became more divergent. Employment and personal incomes fell rapidly and, as the depression spread, more severe international trade and foreign exchange restrictions were imposed.

One result was a sharp decline in motor vehicle exports. The overseas demand for General Motors vehicles produced in the United States and Canada dropped from 250,000 units in 1929 to as little as 44,000 units in 1932—a much sharper decrease than in the company's own volume at home or in total vehicle demand overseas. During this period, General Motors overseas manufacturing facilities helped to stem the decline in overseas sales and by 1935, following an expansion of productive capacity abroad, General Motors had more than recovered its 1929 market share.

The rising importance of overseas manufacturing facilities during these years of economic recovery became increasingly evident. General Motors in 1935 and 1936 supplied about one-quarter of the world market outside the United States and Canada. Over half of these sales were produced in the Opel and Vauxhall plants, as compared with only one-fifth of the company's overseas sales in 1930.

With the economic recovery abroad in the years following 1932, the demand for motor vehicles again expanded rapidly. By 1937, total sales of cars and trucks produced overseas established a new high, about 50 per cent above the level reached in 1929. In contrast to the overall increase in overseas demand, the sales of United States and Canadian source vehicles in overseas countries continued to be depressed by trade restrictions, discriminatory taxes and preferences for locally designed and manufactured products. As a result, the overseas demand for motor vehicles made in the United States and Canada declined by 34 per cent over the same period. The number of cars and trucks exported from the United States and Canada in 1929 was a record which has been unsurpassed since that time.

THE EVOLUTION OF AN OVERSEAS ORGANIZATION

During the twenties and early thirties General Motors developed an overseas organizational structure in step with its changing approach to world markets. This was a period when matters of organization received a great deal of study and experimentation. Even in these early years, corporate management had a concept of organization that gave continuity to General Motors approach in spite of the changing nature of the business and the need for constant adaptation.

Initially, General Motors overseas business was placed under the jurisdiction of the General Motors Export Company established in 1911. In its early years, it was a merchandising organization that took over from the individual manufacturing divisions the responsibility for the sale of all General Motors products outside the United States and Canada. The Export Company was made responsible for the establishment of field offices in overseas territories, and it expanded in size as the business grew. Its function continued to be limited to the sale of products exported from the United States and Canada to overseas distributors.

With the establishment of assembly operations in the twenties, a broader overseas organizational structure was required. This was accomplished by the creation of an Export Group. This larger organizational unit consisted of the individual overseas assembly operations as well as the Export Company.

The Export Group was headed by a Vice President of the Corporation assisted by a staff organized along functional lines. Management coordination and authority flowed through this Vice President from top corporate management to the Export Company, and to the individual assembly plant managers who reported directly to the Vice President.

Assembly plant territories were designated, and the responsibilities of the Export Company for distribution in these territories were transferred to the assembly plant managers. Thus, each assembly plant manager was assigned full operating responsibility for production, distribution and sales in his territory. This pattern was also applied to the manufacturing operations as they became established. Other territories remained under the jurisdiction of the Export Company. This concept of organizing the business on a regional basis has been retained to this day.

By the mid-thirties, the present basic structure of General Motors overseas organization was established. A twofold pattern had emerged. First, overseas operations were administered by a fully integrated operating organization, at the time called the Export Group. Second, each assembly plant and the Export Company were given the responsibility for all of General Motors business in their respective territories. In 1935, the Export Group became the General Motors Overseas Operations Division which included by this time, the two manufacturing subsidiaries—Opel and Vauxhall—as well as the export and assembly operations.

Thus, the overseas organization was adapted to the changing needs of the business in response to the challenges and opportunities provided by growing world markets. While there have been, and will continue to be, many changes in detail reflecting the jobs to be done and the people to do them, two features of this organizational structure deserve emphasis. First, each overseas operation was made an integral part of General Motors as a whole, bearing a relation to the business similar to that of a domestic operating division. Second, in the General Motors approach to serving world markets, the same concepts of organization were applied both at home and overseas. In short, by the mid-thirties, the company had laid the foundation of a world-wide enterprise which went beyond production and distribution to include the management structure of the business and its organization.

OVERSEAS POLICIES DURING THE WAR YEARS

The start of the Second World War closed the decade of depression and recovery overseas. During the War, with its profoundly disrupting effects on world trade and investment patterns, it became apparent that General Motors overseas operations required reevaluation.

Within the General Motors Corporation, the Overseas Policy Group—reporting to what is now the Executive Committee—had been formed near the end of 1936. It was this top policy committee for overseas operations that, during World War II, was charged with the responsibility to study and reexamine all aspects of General Motors operations overseas, including estimates of market potentials and profit prospects after the War.

The studies completed by this policy group during World War II, and the related operating decisions that were reached subsequently, represent what I regard as the third landmark in the evolution of General Motors overseas operations. These studies, optimistic in their outlook and imaginative in their formulation of postwar opportunities, were soundly based on an understanding of the role of the motor vehicle in the major markets of the world. They laid the foundation for the overseas expansion of General Motors in the years after the War.

One of the most significant of these studies projected a rapid expansion of the postwar overseas market for motor vehicles. That the management of General Motors was convinced of a large growth opportunity is evident from the conclusion of a major report to the Overseas Policy Group in July 1944:

> We believe that at some time during the 20-year period following this war, the overseas markets for cars and trucks will at least equal the market in the United States and Canada. We feel that the need for motor transportation of goods and people will be so compelling that the world *will be motorized*—regardless of all problems and obstacles.

As events turned out, it was exactly twenty years later in 1964 that an overseas production of 10.7 million cars and trucks was sufficient to surpass a record year's production of 10.0 million vehicles in the United States and Canada.

The Overseas Policy Group had also anticipated, as

early as 1943, a continuation of the world-wide trend toward industrialization after the War, and had recommended that General Motors contribute to industrial development efforts overseas. Remembering the uncertainties of the war years, a statement of policy approved by the Overseas Policy Group in June of 1943 is of interest:

> General Motors believes that the trends toward industrialization which were observable in many overseas countries before the war will be generally continued and in many cases intensified after the war. . . .
>
> General Motors will participate, through its operating companies abroad, in such phases of local industrial intensification and development as lie within the field of the Corporation's normal domestic activities, automotive or otherwise, and as are considered to be economically and financially sound, technically feasible, and within the potential capacity of the respective General Motors Overseas organizations for effective practical execution. . . .

To carry out our postwar plans, it was reaffirmed that General Motors operations outside the United States and Canada would continue to be the responsibility of the Overseas Operations Division within the framework of overall corporate policy. The responsibility for making overseas policy recommendations continues to be vested in the Overseas Policy

Group. This group, an arm of the Executive Committee, has drawn its membership from members of the Executive Committee, Overseas Operations Division executives, and other top corporate officers. In this, it reflects a conviction growing out of our experience that our overseas operations must be fully integrated parts of General Motors if they are to serve their markets efficiently. While our individual subsidiaries have been, and continue to be, tailored specifically to the needs of each economy, General Motors remains a single world-wide enterprise in concept, organization, structure and operation.

DECENTRALIZED OPERATIONS WITH COORDINATED CONTROL

To attain unity and adaptability, two broad operating principles, adopted some forty-five years ago, have been of fundamental importance to General Motors. These are the principles of decentralized operating responsibility with clearly defined line authority and coordinated policy control through the use of centralized staff functions. These apply to both domestic and overseas operations.

The concept of decentralized operations and responsibilities with coordinated policy control appears, at first blush, to contain an inherent inconsistency. The goal itself is clear. The objective is to create an organization that can adjust to different and changing circumstances. This is intended to give a maximum of freedom and incentive for individual initiative and, at the same time, to realize the efficiencies and the economies inherent in a closely coordinated operation. In line with this, top management has the responsibility for formulating and administering policies applicable to the business as a whole, while operating responsibility is assigned to the individual operating division or subsidiary within the limits set by overall policy.

The formulation of overall policies and the setting of strategic goals for the business as a whole can only provide direction markers for each line executive who has the responsibility to manage his own part of the business. These direction markers do not automatically dictate operating decisions. They can only be guides to the line executive whose experience, skill and understanding of the full implications of the policy are critical.

For this reason, General Motors attaches the highest importance to the selection of its managers both in the United States and overseas. They must know and understand policy. They must know the policy limits of their authority. They must recognize when a decision might breach these limits and require a policy determination. The concept of operating decentralization and policy coordination is only as effective as the people who administer it, and their effectiveness depends on years of experience in the day-to-day operation of the business.

The scheduling of production is a good example of the interplay of factors in the coordination of decentralized operations. It is corporate policy to establish production schedules to meet a number of objectives. The level of production must be closely geared to market requirements. Dealers must be provided with an adequate inventory of cars reflecting both the level of demand and the variety of product. Consistent with meeting these objectives, a maximum stability of employment must be maintained. These are, in the scheduling area of the business, the direction markers.

The establishment of production goals to meet these policy objectives is the responsibility of top corporate management, assisted by the central office staffs, and with the consultation of division managers. Responsibility for the policy and its translation into a set of production objectives for each division and the overall business cannot be delegated. It involves an understanding of each part of the business in relation to the business as a whole. Top corporate management must consider the production capacity of the manufacturing subsidiaries in relation to that of the assembly facilities, the availability of supplies and materials, and the allocation of production capacity among the divisions and subsidiaries. It must consider the implications of the effect of these production schedules on the employees. It must assess objectives in terms of the financial requirements of the business. It must be aware of, and prepared for, possible changes in the market in order to respond quickly when they occur. Over the longer term, it must plan for expansion and have an overall view of where new investment may yield the highest return to the business.

Once production objectives have been established, the divisional or subsidiary management has the responsibility for determining how these objectives can best be achieved. In what proportions will the many models and body styles be ordered and produced? What combinations of color and interior trim will be specified, and which materials must be obtained now? Which design improvements can be introduced? Where can manufacturing efficiency be improved? These and countless other operating responsibilities are delegated to the line executives in the divisions and the subsidiaries to be carried out within the broad production objectives established.

The concept of decentralized operations and responsibilities with coordinated policy control has proved to be particularly important in our overseas operations. On the one hand, our manufacturing and assembly facilities are bound together on a continuing, almost daily, basis by the economics of producing, assembling and distributing vehicles. These closely interrelated activities must be coordinated within a unifying policy framework to achieve maximum efficiency. On the other hand, each overseas plant manager must adapt his operation to the legal and market requirements of the national economy he serves. These requirements demand the flexibility of decentralization.

LINE AND STAFF

The General Motors concept of decentralized but coordinated responsibilities required fresh thinking about the form of organization which would best achieve our objectives. To this end, General Motors at an early date adopted a line and staff principle. Line executives, whether assigned in the United States, Canada or overseas, were given full operating responsibility and authority within established policy limits. This assured the flexibility necessary to adapt individual operations to local conditions, and to adjust operations quickly as local conditions changed.

Application of the staff principle resulted in modifications which took two directions. First, emphasis was placed on the creation of central staffs that would complement the staffs at the divisional or subsidiary levels. Second, the responsibilities of these central staffs were expanded beyond the traditional advisory functions to include policy coordination for the business as a whole within their special areas. Over the years, a number of central staffs have been created including such staffs as sales, engineering, manufacturing, personnel, public relations and finance. Each staff is under the direction of a General Motors Vice President, and each supports and receives policy guidance from a policy group composed of top corporate officers.

The central staffs supply technical services to all operating divisions, and where there are complementary divisional staffs there is a close working relationship. Moreover, the coordinating functions of our central staffs hold a prominent place in their activities. For example, public relations policies are recommended at the central staff level. When formulated by the Personnel and Public Relations Policy Group and approved by the Executive Committee, they are applicable to General Motors as a whole and are administered at the division or subsidiary level. Financial policies are established by the Finance Committee on recommendation from the Financial Staff. In this case, in order to assure coordinated and uniform financial control and reporting, each divisional and subsidiary comptroller is responsible both to his general manager and to the Comptroller of the Corporation.

In short, General Motors has in its adaptation of the line and staff principle, a form of organization which is a logical counterpart of decentralized operations with coordinated policy control. In this form of organization both the line and the staff play key roles. Each would be unproductive without the other.

OPERATING OVERSEAS

Unlike our domestic business, where manufacturing and assembly functions are in close proximity or tied together by fast and dependable transportation, great distances often separate overseas manufacture and assembly. The Opel components, which in disassembled form are shipped from General Motors plants in West Germany, may reach our Port Elizabeth plant in South Africa for assembly some three and a half weeks later. This is only one shipment from one source. If the South African assembly operation and its recently added manufacturing facilities are to function smoothly and efficiently, they must today receive a carefully controlled and coordinated flow of vehicle parts and components from West Germany, England, Canada, the United States and even Australia. These must reach General Motors South African in the right volume and at the right time to allow an orderly scheduling of assembly without accumulation of excessive inventories. This is a challenging assignment which must be made to work if the investment is to be a profitable one.

Differences in language, in monetary units, in laws governing the operation of a business, in labor availability and in the skill and motivation of the labor force must be recognized in every overseas operation. Adaptation to these differences is critically important to the successful performance of the business, day in and day out.

It is expected that our corporate officers will have an understanding of our overseas operating problems. In my own case, it has been my practice to supplement my participation in the Overseas Policy Group with first-hand observations of our operations around the world. I consider this essential to an understanding of our overseas problems.

Overall operating authority and responsibility for General Motors business outside the United States and Canada, on a day-to-day basis, is assigned to the General Manager of the Overseas Operations Division. Part of his authority, in turn, is delegated through a Director of the Opel, Vauxhall and Holden's Group to the Managing Directors of these three largest overseas manufacturing subsidiaries. In the case of other overseas operating units, his authority flows through home office Regional Group Executives and Regional Managers to the Managing Directors of these units, with each level of responsibility and operating authority being defined in terms of a geographic area.

Unlike many of our other divisions, and reflecting the unusual character and diversity of problems, the Overseas Operations Division has extensive home office staff functions located in New York and Detroit. They perform in the same manner as the central office staffs of the Corporation, providing technical services, coordinating the work of the Division, initiating proposals and assuring, through liaison with the central office staffs, coordination and continuity of policy between General Motors domestic and overseas operations.

Through these staff activities, the closest possible contact is maintained among the overseas subsidiaries, the home office of the Overseas Operations Division and the General Motors Corporation central office. The overseas subsidiary, working through the home office staff of the Overseas Operations Division, can draw on the central office staff facilities of General Motors for the benefit of a broader experience that is concerned with both domestic and overseas problems. The process of internal exchange and consultation often involves a close working relationship among the technical staffs of the various overseas subsidiaries. Particularly in this postwar period, operating overseas has meant growing overseas. In meeting this challenge, the balanced perspective which results from a decentralization of operating responsibility coordinated within a framework of basic policy has been invaluable in helping us to see the opportunity ahead.

Keeping in mind our long experience both at home and abroad, I do not wish to underestimate the contribution of a sound organizational structure. On the other hand, I would not wish to convey an impression that seems to overemphasize its role in determining the overall performance of the enterprise. I would stress the point that while organizational principles, basic policies and the procedures of decision-making must be logically consistent with the needs of the business in a constantly changing world, they do not and can not stand alone.

Principles, policies and procedures are effective only insofar as the management of an enterprise understands them and relates them in a meaningful way to the day-to-day operations of the business. Application is the key, and accomplishment is the final test. In the case of General Motors, I believe that the soundness of the methods of operation has been confirmed by the results.

As I look back over the past half century during which General Motors emerged as a world-wide industrial enterprise, I am impressed by three major landmarks in this evolution. These were, in my opinion, the decision to establish assembly facilities overseas, the decision to manufacture abroad and, finally, the group of decisions made during the Second World War to expand operations in key areas to meet a rapidly growing world market for motor vehicles. These decisions provide the background for an understanding of General Motors postwar competitive strategy. This is developed more fully in the next chapter which deals with four of our most important postwar strategic decisions.

3

THE STRATEGY OF
A WORLD-WIDE OPERATION

TODAY'S WORLD MARKETS

The decisions of General Motors reached during the years before 1945 set the stage for our postwar expansion overseas. In these years, we came to realize an even more urgent need for the flexibility of decentralized operations responsive to local conditions within a framework of unified policy control.

Reduced to fundamentals, three characteristics of world markets can be identified as importantly affecting our postwar competitive strategy. The first element is diversity. A snapshot of the world today would reveal a procession of national economies at varying stages of development, extending from the most primitive economic arrangements to advanced industrial societies. Each economy differs from every other in the character of its markets and the requirements for serving the public. These differences must be recognized and accommodated in mapping out an effective motor vehicle manufacturing and distribution system on a world-wide basis.

A second element is the rapid pace of change both within and among these national economies. Shifts in the terms of trade among nations tend to expand international buying power in some countries, while reducing it in others. National efforts to conserve supplies of foreign exchange and reduce imports can rapidly alter trade patterns. National monetary and fiscal policies, through their effects on domestic production, incomes and prices often play a significant role in determining international trade and investment activity.

A third reality of world business—and one that distinguishes it most clearly from domestic business—is the variety of goals of independent sovereign nations. The policies, attitudes toward private enterprise and receptivity to world trade and investment set each nation apart, to some degree, from all the others. Each national economy has a distinctive quality and its market is, correspondingly, a distinctive challenge.

Within the context of these fundamentals of world markets, General Motors worked out its postwar competitive strategy. The forces influencing world industrialization and the growth in motor vehicle demand were studied carefully in each nation to determine the operational requirements for doing business on a world-wide basis. In almost every month during the postwar period, our policy-making groups have examined and weighed specific proposals affecting the development of our overseas operations.

To illustrate our approach to overseas expansion, I have selected four major General Motors decisions from our postwar experience—the decision to resume the operating control of Opel in West Germany, the decision to manufacture vehicles in Australia, the decision to expand to a full-line production of passenger cars in England and West Germany, and the group of decisions to begin vehicle manufacturing programs in some of the developing countries. Each of these had its own features. Taken together, they provide a good indication of the range of considerations required for successful competition in the world motor vehicle market.

THE POSTWAR CHALLENGE OF PRODUCTION OVERSEAS

The first and overriding requirement of the immediate postwar years was to supply vehicles to a world that was starved for transportation, whether or not the price could immediately be paid. Overseas motor vehicle manufacturing capacity had been converted to war production, and much of it had been seriously damaged.

The motor vehicle industry in the United States and Canada met these needs by stepping up exports as rapidly as possible consistent with fulfilling demands at home and with the historical role of exports in the overall distribution of our cars and trucks. In the first three years following 1945, two-fifths of the new vehicles sold overseas came from manufacturing sources in the United States and Canada.

General Motors energetically promoted its overseas business in these years. To fill the immediate overseas demands for our vehicles on the most efficient basis possible, we relied heavily on our overseas assembly facilities. This gave us additional assembly capacity at a time when our home facilities were stretched tight. Even more important in terms of General Motors long-term postwar growth, our overseas assembly facilities became focal points around which our dealer and service networks were reestablished.

Although the export of vehicle components with assembly overseas was the best possible approach to meet the emergency conditions in the years immediately after the Second World War, in the long run it could not be competitive with locally produced vehicles overseas. Accordingly, the Vauxhall plant in England, which had been bombed in 1940 but not destroyed, was brought back into civilian production of trucks for commercial use in November 1945, only three months after the Japanese surrender. By January 1946, passenger cars began to roll off the Vauxhall lines.

The decision with respect to Opel was more difficult because General Motors had not been in control of this operation since 1940. Immediately following the War, the remaining Opel facilities in West Germany came under the jurisdiction of Allied occupation forces. The plant had been extensively damaged.

Many of the prewar tools, dies and fixtures—in one case the entire set of tools to manufacture a popular model—had been either removed or destroyed. The decision to resume control and initiate commercial production at Opel in 1948 was preceded by a searching examination that included an on-the-spot study in March of that year by a group of executives, of which I was a member, sent from this country.

The question of resuming control of Opel was not easily resolved. Considering the many uncertainties surrounding operations in Germany in the early postwar period, this was understandable. In the final analysis, three factors were persuasive to our group. First, despite heavy destruction of the plant, basic facilities needed to resume limited production were available. We could foresee that if the German monetary system were reformed, sufficient funds for full reconstruction of the plant could be generated by the Opel enterprise itself. This was very important because General Motors own corporate resources, already stretched thin by needs in the United States, could not have been subjected to substantial and additional demands at that time.

Second, our group was confident that the market for motor vehicles in West Germany and on the continent of Western Europe would grow as reconstruction advanced and as international political and economic relations stabilized.

Third, our network of overseas assembly facilities was a resource which required the support of a full-scale manufacturing operation strategically located on the European continent. It was clear from our discussions with Allied and West German officials that our commercial interest in expanding exports meshed well with national economic objectives. At no time in my personal experience with General Motors was the essential interdependence between each part of the business and the whole more sharply brought into focus than during this period.

It was this combination of factors that impelled me, as well as the other members of the group, to urge that General Motors formally resume operating control of Opel. This was accomplished late in 1948.

With the resumption of production at Opel and Vauxhall, the prewar pattern of competitive strategy was reestablished. Overseas sales of United States and Canadian source vehicles continued to be hampered by trade and exchange restrictions, discriminatory taxes and a general preference overseas for locally designed and manufactured products. The reemergence of our overseas manufacturing capability allowed us to compete with other overseas vehicle manufacturers whose products were specifically designed for European markets. Our overseas assembly plants could now draw on General Motors output in England and West Germany as well as in the United States and Canada to meet the demands for these products through our world-wide network of dealers established in the prewar years.

Toward the end of the forties, General Motors had again reached a point where we could profitably compete for the markets we had cultivated before the War. It is no overstatement to say that this was achieved because our broad plans had been soundly made before the close of the War so that we were prepared to meet opportunities and problems as they arose.

EMBARKING ON A NEW VENTURE IN AUSTRALIA

The importance of an overall policy approach is well illustrated by a second decision, reached in the mid-forties, to undertake—for the first time on the part of any business enterprise—the volume manufacture of a passenger car in Australia. In line with the earlier policy directive to participate in world-wide industrial advance, the Overseas Policy Group had reached the decision, in September 1944, ". . . that General Motors' activities in Australia should be closely identified with the future course of industrial development in that country."

We were none too soon in reaching this decision. The very next month the government of Australia addressed a communication to our Australian assembly plant—General Motors–Holden's—asking the company to indicate whether it would be interested in manufacturing a motor car in Australia and, if the answer were affirmative, to submit a proposal at our earliest convenience for the government's consideration. Other manufacturers received the same communication.

We were fortunate that a detailed study of this question had already been completed. Within fifteen days it was possible to provide the Overseas Policy Group with a report summarizing the situation. I can do no better than quote a portion of this report which sets out the economic and business factors considered by the Group.

> There are several governing factors which have led us to the conclusion that we should move in the direction of complete motor car manufacture in Australia:
>
> First, it is our opinion that the potential market is sufficiently large to support a motor car manufacturing program. . . .
>
> Second, Australia has the industrial background necessary to support a car manufacturing program. . . .
>
> Third, detailed analyses indicate that a car with requirements satisfactory to the Australian market can be manufactured economically and that, in fact,

it can be produced at costs substantially under the landed cost of corresponding imported cars.

Fourth, the Australian government strongly supports a car manufacturing program in Australia. . . .

Finally, we believe General Motors can undertake a manufacturing program along lines which will enable us to earn a satisfactory return on the investment, which will meet the requirements of lower cost to the consumer, and which will provide a car more suitable to Australia's needs. Furthermore, we believe that such a program will enable us to improve our strong position in the Australian market by increasing our share of the total available business.

On the other hand, it is our opinion that if we do not undertake a manufacturing program our position in Australia will become weakened. . . . We believe that with only imported products to fall back upon and with government support of competitive local manufacture, we would operate in a shrinking market area and face a steadily declining share of the total market.

The fact that we had been able to satisfy ourselves on these considerations made it possible for us to submit a detailed proposal to the Australian government within three months—in January of 1945. This proposal was based on a number of key factors in General Motors overseas planning. Let me quote the relevant parts of the General Motors proposal.

With respect to the product, we indicated that:

The World-wide Industrial Enterprise

We would undertake to manufacture in Australia a five seater sedan car and related utility [a small passenger and cargo-carrying vehicle] which would be specially designed for the economic and operating conditions of Australia.

With respect to competition, we stated first, that:

The objective of General Motors–Holden's Ltd. is to manufacture Australian motor vehicles in the low price group to sell competitively with imported vehicles without subsidy and without increase in the customs tariff rate prevailing in 1939.

Moreover, we made it clear that:

General Motors–Holden's does not request that any special advantages be extended to them. . . . It is believed by General Motors–Holden's that an efficient automotive industry, providing low cost, satisfactory quality transportation to the Australian public can best be established under free competitive conditions. . . .

This recognizes that any other concern will be equally free to enter into manufacture of any type under the same conditions as are accorded by the Government to General Motors–Holden's.

Finally, the benefits which General Motors worldwide operation could bring to the development of an Australian motor vehicle industry—through the close relationship between the proposed manufacturing subsidiary and the parent company—were set out as follows:

Arrangements have been made which will enable General Motors–Holden's to procure from General Motors Corporation manufacturing rights, including processes, drawings, specifications, and other technical data. The services of General Motors Corporation engineers in specialized branches will be made available to General Motors–Holden's and General Motors–Holden's Ltd. engineers will have access to General Motors Corporation factories in the United States, Canada and England to observe and familiarize themselves first hand with manufacturing methods and processes. Such assistance and advice from General Motors Corporation will be continued to assure General Motors–Holden's of a constant flow of technical information on the latest developments of automotive design, manufacture and research.

A number of points emerge from this proposal to initiate motor vehicle manufacturing in Australia. First, from the beginning of General Motors participation in Australia on an import and assembly basis, the Australian market for motor vehicles had been highly competitive. Since the Australian government had addressed its request to a number of world-wide manufacturers, the chances were that if we did not accept the challenge, some other manufacturer would. In short, if we failed to move toward manufacturing in Australia, we stood to lose all or a major part of our market in that part of the world. The extent and durability of this competitive climate is illustrated by the fact that in Australia today there are five major companies manufacturing passenger cars in whole or in part locally, and six primary producers of commercial vehicles.

Second, in the view of General Motors the proposal was an economic one. Local industries to which General Motors could turn for materials, components and services were in existence, and with the stimulus provided by our participation, they would be encouraged to expand. The market potential was expected to support a manufacturing facility. Most important, at the demand levels we anticipated, we were able to conclude that a vehicle attractive to the Australian market could be supplied at a lower cost than a not-so-well adapted vehicle could be imported.

Third, General Motors was able to undertake this venture because its world-wide resources of design, engineering and manufacturing skill could be brought to the development of a distinctive Australian car. This resource made the risk an acceptable one to us and, in my judgment, was largely responsible for the acceptance of our product when it was introduced in 1948.

Adding up these factors, General Motors concluded that this proposal could stand on its own feet economically and competitively. There were a number of good reasons for our entering the Australian market. They were so persuasive that we moved ahead with a manufacturing program.

Let me summarize what that decision has meant. In October of 1944, when our initial postwar project to develop manufacturing operations in Australia was being considered, we felt that we could safely plan for the manufacture of at least 20,000 motor vehicles a year by 1950. Australian manufacture of General Motors vehicles began with 163 Holden cars late in 1948 and, as projected, two years later in 1950 slightly over 20,000 Holden cars and trucks were produced.

With the subsequent expansion of the Australian economy, the growth of supplying industries, an expanding dealer network and a policy of reinvesting a substantial part of the earnings of General Motors–Holden's in additional plant and equipment, it was possible for this facility in early 1966 to produce at a rate in excess of 200,000 units per year. Today, Holden's is not only an effective competitor for domestic business, but it also competes aggressively for export sales worldwide through the assembly and distribution network established and maintained by General Motors.

THE EVOLUTION OF FULL-LINE COMPETITION

The third major development illustrative of General Motors postwar competitive strategy was the decision to expand the line of passenger cars produced in West Germany and England from one serving only a part of the market to a full line. This was under study during the last half of the fifties, and the final decision was reached in 1960.

The growth in motor vehicle ownership and use in Europe in the nineteen fifties closely tracked the rate of growth in the United States in the twenties. Therefore, it did not come as a surprise that in the fifties, as in the United States thirty years earlier, our attention was directed toward evaluating the manufacturing economies and marketing efficiencies of full-line operations overseas. However, the General Motors motto of the early nineteen twenties—"A Car for Every Purse and Purpose"—was not achieved in England and Germany until the early nineteen sixties.

In the United States of the twenties General Motors recognized that, with the growth in the size of the market, customer preferences would become increasingly diverse, reflecting a greater variety in the use of cars as well as differences in individual tastes and incomes. It was apparent that these varied preferences could be served most efficiently by producers who offered a full line of cars. More effective use could be made of established central staffs. For example, with the larger volume of sales possible with a full line, extensive research, engineering and styling facilities could be supported. The work of these groups could be made available for improving the entire line. Similarly, specialized services in the fields of product testing, manufacturing methods, marketing and finance could be provided, thus contributing to greater efficiency. Full-line production also meant a larger volume base permitting additional unit cost reductions for many parts and components used in all vehicles.

In the mid-fifties General Motors products manufactured in West Germany and England were competitive in only the upper part of the European and English domestic markets. The prewar tools, dies and fixtures required for a smaller car had been removed from West Germany before we resumed control of Opel. The middle and upper segments of the market were expanding, and we were heavily engaged in enlarging our capacity to serve these profitable markets. During this period we kept the question of producing a smaller car in West Germany under continuous study, but it was not until later in the decade that we could see our way to realizing the potential in the remaining lower part of the car market.

At the same time the motorization of Europe, which we had foreseen in 1944, was rapidly becoming a reality. With rising incomes, a steadily increasing number of families was moving toward ownership of a small car. The bicycle rack, for years a standard feature of European plants, was giving way to parking lots filled with small cars with one-liter engines. The demand for vehicles of this type was further intensified by the lack of a large supply of used cars which had become an important factor in the United States, particularly in the postwar years.

In the late nineteen fifties, General Motors design and engineering staffs in West Germany and in England independently began to develop prototypes of the smaller one-liter car. At the same time, intensive investigations were undertaken to locate possible new plant sites in both countries. Further detailed studies of the market potentials in West Germany, England and export areas, for a newly designed smaller car, were also conducted.

It became increasingly clear that if General Motors could produce a small vehicle of the one-liter class which could be sold at a competitive price, there was a demand potential—one that gave every indication of growing as fast or faster than the rest of the overseas market. The factor over which General Motors had some control was the design of the car. If this proved acceptable to our customers, certain volume assumptions could be made and, on this basis, cost estimates developed.

Therefore, design of the vehicle became the critical element. Every effort was made to improve on existing designs that were competitive in this portion of the market. During the two years prior to the introduction of the cars, the design and manufacturing staffs in the

United States and at Opel and Vauxhall worked together while the styling staffs in both West Germany and England individually developed styling and performance modifications suited to each market. These cars—the Opel Kadett and the Vauxhall Viva—were introduced in 1962 and 1963, respectively, and met with immediate customer approval.

Another critical element in the expansion of our manufacturing facilities in West Germany and England was plant location. Pockets of unemployment prevailed within generally tight labor markets in the two countries at this time, and national economic policies were encouraging investment in these areas. As always, we also had to consider plant location in terms of manufacturing and marketing efficiency. Reflecting such considerations, our expansion in West Germany, for example, resulted in the construction of a new manufacturing and assembly plant at Bochum in 1962. This furnished an expansion of employment opportunity in a coal mining area in the Ruhr containing a number of displaced workers. Today, our Opel plant at Bochum provides employment for some 15,000 people.

Related facilities necessary for the manufacture of motor vehicles were also enlarged at Opel and Vauxhall following the decision to add the one-liter car to our world-wide product offering. In the context of the

59

complementary relationships maintained within the General Motors organization, the styling and engineering facilities in both our Opel and Vauxhall operations were greatly expanded and, today, their automotive design and technical capabilities are fully consistent with the modern demands of the markets they serve.

Expansion of the capacity to produce the one-liter car at Opel and Vauxhall is continuing. In Germany, by the end of the 1966 model year, the Kadett will account for 42 per cent of the total productive capacity of Opel. In England, by mid-1967, the Viva will represent 47 per cent of Vauxhall's total capacity. And, in Australia, Holden's is planning to expand the locally manufactured content of the one-liter Viva to 95 per cent by the end of 1969. With these new cars, General Motors is in a position to compete in about 90 per cent of the product range in these overseas markets; and General Motors dealers throughout the overseas world have a much broader product base for their sales and service responsibilities and opportunities.

Similarly, the export markets served by Opel and Vauxhall have been strengthened. General Motors assembly and distribution facilities can now offer a markedly new and substantially expanded range of products to our dealers and customers. Including the lines produced in the United States and Canada in the 1966 model year, our customers around the world had a choice of buying passenger cars ranging from under 155 inches to over 244 inches in overall length and with curb weights extending from about 1,600 pounds to over 5,600 pounds. It is this capacity of a world-wide producer to serve highly varied automotive demands that is a great source of strength. For General Motors this has been a key factor in competitive strategy since our first overseas investments were made in the twenties.

ACCELERATED INDUSTRIALIZATION IN DEVELOPING COUNTRIES

Viewed in terms of the competitive strategy and tactics of world-wide industrial companies, the previous General Motors examples contain most of the elements of the classic cases in which, in serving the requirements of the market, economic considerations of efficiency have been closely geared to the needs of the national economy. There are many variations in these patterns, and a long-range strategic plan for world market participation must be responsive to them.

In our own case, these variations have been most commonly associated with the programs of accelerated industrialization being carried forward in the developing countries outside Europe and Australia. While each of these countries has had its own separate and often distinctive program, there are many common elements.

First, the requirement for local motor vehicle manufacture is generally a matter of stated national policy.

Second, to achieve the stated objective, each manufacturer in the country is asked to agree to increase the percentage of the vehicle produced locally. Implementing legislation and decrees usually establish a timetable of required increases, with penalty duties levied on the parts of the car still imported if the schedule is not met. Very high duties are generally levied on any import of completely assembled vehicles.

Third, the immediate and near-term market potential in these countries is generally small reflecting the early stages of industrialization and low per capita income.

Since the effect of these national policies is to put each vehicle producer, who seeks to participate, in the position of becoming a local manufacturer, the result is that a relatively small market is served by a number of manufacturers with each on a low volume basis. From an economic point of view, the market might well be served more efficiently in some other way—generally through importing all, or a relatively high percentage of, vehicle parts and components with reliance upon local assembly operations to secure maximum cost savings. However, development along these lines is barred by prohibitive penalty duties. Clearly, these are instances where competitive strategy is influenced importantly by national policy.

General Motors has had long-established assembly facilities in many of the countries that are now accelerating vehicle manufacture. With these facilities we have realized the economies of high volume component manufacture in Germany, England, Australia and North America combined with local assembly and distribution of vehicles. Therefore, the basic strategic question which we had to face in each instance was whether General Motors should continue to participate with a manufacturing operation which, in view of the limited market, would be less efficient, or to liquidate its investment in assembly facilities and withdraw from the market. In each instance, resolution of this issue has depended on whether General Motors could foresee a growth potential in which its investments could earn a satisfactory profit in a competitive market.

Within the past ten years, General Motors has had to face up to this question in a number of the industrializing countries. In several, we did not elect to develop local manufacturing facilities. In four countries, however, manufacture of motor vehicles is now an established fact, or well along to becoming so. Although the program in each of these countries has distinctive features, let me illustrate our approach by specific reference to the factors influencing our decision to expand our assembly operation into a manufacturing facility in Argentina.

Before World War II, Argentina was one of our best export markets outside Europe. Our plant in Argentina, established in 1925, originally assembled passenger cars and trucks from parts manufactured in our United States plants. By 1958, General Motors automotive operations in Argentina included the sale of passenger cars from West Germany and the United States, and the assembly of Bedford trucks from Vauxhall in England. We also had facilities for the manufacture of batteries and springs.

As part of our overall review of overseas operations during World War II, the Overseas Policy Group had concluded that in Argentina motor vehicle assembly rather than manufacturing would be more economically sound in the postwar years. Although Argentina was pushing forward with general industrial expansion, it was anticipated that the country would be limited by the lack of strong supporting industries and by a shortage of essential raw materials and natural resources such as iron, coal, lumber and waterpower. The available labor force was excellent, but the long-term outlook as expressed in our review was that Argentina's industrial development would be advanced more rapidly and economically by continued reliance on an operation which combined the economies of local vehicle assembly with the efficiencies of outside parts and component manufacture.

However, in 1958 and early 1959, Argentina moved rapidly in the direction of requiring local manufacture, and General Motors was forced to reconsider the nature of its operations. Prohibitive import restrictions, imposed by the Argentine government in January of 1959, would bring the importation and assembly of all vehicles to a halt. For example, a standard Chevrolet passenger car selling under $2,500 in the United States would have cost over $20,000, including duty and surcharges, in Argentina.

Two months later in March of 1959, the government of Argentina published a decree which set forth its intent to develop a local automotive manufacturing industry within a five-year period and established the conditions under which this was to be accomplished. Any company proposing to participate in the automotive market in Argentina was first required to produce a minimum of 40 per cent of the vehicle locally (based on the value of cost and freight) and by January 1, 1963, to produce the engine locally. For manufacturers with approved programs, the Argentine government held out the inducements of duty-free entry of new machinery, tools and equipment; protection against imported products through surcharge schedules favorable to local manufacturers; and official permission to transfer the annual net profits earned on investment through the free exchange market. For General Motors, and for a number of other vehicle producers, the question was whether to manufacture in Argentina or abandon that market.

We made this decision in the affirmative. We moved ahead with a manufacturing program, first for commercial vehicles and then for passenger cars. Our willingness to participate in the accelerated industrialization program of Argentina reflected primarily our desire to retain a position in a market which, given this framework of declared national policy, appeared to be a reasonable risk from a profit point of view. We could foresee the possibility of an improving long-term potential. We concluded that national policies would be conducive to private enterprise. It was our expectation that the investment in expanded plant facilities could be accomplished without any considerable dollar outflow from the United States relying, in part, upon earnings generated within Argentina, and in part, upon the shipment of machinery and equipment from our United States operations in return for capital stock of the Argentine subsidiary. Furthermore, we anticipated the development of local supplying industries necessary for motor vehicle manufacturing.

Our investment in manufacturing capacity in the

Argentine should be distinguished from our decision to manufacture vehicles in Australia. The Australian investment was economic in terms of greater manufacturing efficiency, more suitable product design and lower unit costs over a period of years. A similar investment in manufacturing facilities in Argentina could not be as readily defended. As sound as such a program may prove to be in the long run, for the foreseeable future it exacts a penalty in terms of reduced efficiency and higher prices to the Argentine customer.

While I have used Argentina as illustrative of one approach taken by the developing countries, I would not want to leave the impression that this particular pattern has been imposed without variation in other areas. At present, we are manufacturing vehicles in Brazil, Mexico and the Republic of South Africa as well as Argentina. Each decision required the consideration of our present and prospective position in the market, varying market opportunities and widely different regulations governing investment and trade. Brazilian truck production began in 1959. Passenger car and truck production in Argentina started in 1963. In Mexico and the Republic of South Africa, we have recently added the manufacture of engines and other components, but still continue to import body stampings for our passenger cars.

67

In each of these four countries, the development of manufacturing facilities was an extension of an assembly operation. A distribution network had already been established, and General Motors products had achieved a recognized place in the market. Moreover, the assembly operation had provided a financial base for meeting the additional investment from retained earnings and local borrowing.

As a manufacturer, our preference is to serve all markets on the most efficient basis possible. The fact that national policies often have the initial consequence of raising motor vehicle costs and prices has offset, at least temporarily, some of the stimulating effects which are associated with expanding motor vehicle use, and thus far has foreclosed to these countries some of the manufacturing and distribution economies inherent in the assembly plant approach.

Our own position is clearly defined. It is the responsibility of each country to establish those policies which it deems will serve its interests best. It is then our business responsibility to judge whether we can operate profitably within the framework of this national policy. This is a responsibility which requires a most careful weighing of alternatives. More importantly, it requires a willingness to take a long view of the prospects—both within the market and in relation to the overall goals of the business world-wide.

Moreover, our position does not end with the initial decisions but must be reassessed on a periodic basis. As has been so evident during the two decades since the end of World War II, industrial and economic progress in the developing countries does not follow an even course. The fact that industrialization is under "forced draft" often results in inflationary pressure. The demands of labor for higher money wages often contribute to this. Monetary stability is sometimes lacking. Often political institutions are not stable. In short, there are special risks in these areas which must be weighed, and reweighed, against what is generally a favorable appraisal of the long-term opportunity.

SEEKING BASIC POLICIES FOR PARTICIPATION IN WORLD MARKETS

General Motors experience illustrates the great diversity of the challenges facing a world-wide enterprise. The business objective of using resources profitably cannot depend upon a rigid unyielding point of view in each national market. On the contrary, the approach must be responsive to the stern realities of world competition, to the goals of national policy and to the constantly changing climate of world economic development.

Confronted by the unceasing, restless ebb and flow

of trade and the shifting pressures of national attitudes, it is easy for a business to lose touch with its underlying policy and to improvise. This imposes a continuing obligation on management to reexamine its policies periodically in the light of changing conditions in the world economy.

In General Motors we have tried to keep these facts constantly in mind while at the same time exploring new ways to assure that our activities are closely identified with the development of each national economy in which we operate. To this end, I established in 1960 a National Identification Committee to make a continuing reexamination of our overseas operating policies and positions. The Committee members— top officers from the Overseas Division and the central office staff—completed their first report to the Board of Directors in 1961.

That report was based upon a careful review of the changing nature of our operations outside the United States and the changing nature of the world environment. It included summaries of surveys covering a wide range of subjects such as national attitudes toward investment by United States companies, the approach of firms in the United States to overseas investment, employment and ownership policy.

I will touch on three of the Committee's recommendations, reserving for the next chapter a more thorough examination of their implementation.

First, it was concluded that our long-standing policy of maintaining complete ownership of our operating subsidiaries was essential to the efficient world operation of General Motors, and remained as compelling as it had ever been. During the postwar period, the forces of world competition in motor vehicles had greatly intensified with advancing industrialization. The world, particularly the Western world, was moving toward much closer economic ties. National markets were being consolidated into larger regional markets in Europe and South America, and in North America already close ties were being strengthened. In our view, these basic trends toward integration of product markets reinforced the requirements of a unified ownership point of view.

Second, the Committee found a growing desire in many countries for ownership participation in General Motors and its subsidiaries. This desire, I might add, had been made very clear to me in conversations with government and business leaders overseas.

The interest in ownership participation was one that I could understand completely. We had done everything possible to assure that each General Motors overseas subsidiary had become an integral part of the economic life of the country. We found a growing awareness among local leaders of the contribution each subsidiary was making. That the overseas subsidiary often provided an attractive investment opportunity was also clear. At the same time, I was impressed by the fact that a great many overseas business and political leaders recognized that the profitableness of the subsidiary resulted from the close integration of the subsidiary with the business as a whole.

With these considerations in mind, the Committee recommended a policy of using General Motors resources even more fully than in the past to stimulate the sale overseas of General Motors common stock. Implementation of this policy came to involve efforts to extend the availability of our financial reports to potential investors around the world and additional efforts to extend the listing and availability of General Motors stock in overseas countries. In my judgment, this policy to encourage a wider base of ownership could well prove to be as significant for the future growth of the business world-wide as the three earlier landmark decisions relating to General Motors overseas assembly, manufacture and expansion policy.

Third, the Committee reaffirmed the intent of General Motors to continue the policy of maximum employment of citizens of the country in which the subsidiary is located, to provide the means for their growth and to advance qualified national employees to top executive positions and to the boards of directors of the subsidiaries. In my work with overseas subsidiaries, I have come to know well and to have the highest regard for the skill and dedication of our overseas employees, so this policy is one which has had my unqualified support. In early 1966, citizens of overseas countries, who were high level operating executives and board members of General Motors overseas subsidiaries, constituted about 40 per cent of the total membership of these subsidiary boards.

The search continues in General Motors for effective business policies and strategies appropriately suited to the changing characteristics of the motor vehicle industry, the changing demands of world markets and the dynamics of world competition. A major goal continues to give direction to our policies and strategies today—that is, to find ways by which each subsidiary operation can be more fully integrated into the economic life of its country. Reinforcing this is a second goal to enhance the contribution the subsidiary can make to its national economy by integrating its activity as fully as possible into the business as a whole, thereby permitting it to draw on the larger resources of the world-wide enterprise.

I believe that these would be two of the basic goals of every effective and successful multi-national industrial firm. To the extent that they are achieved, the business will be serving its owners, employees and customers in every country where it operates.

As I look back with the benefit of hindsight on the development of our competitive strategy and tactics and on operating decisions in which I have been involved on a day-to-day basis, I can naturally see instances where General Motors might have done things differently with possibly better results. Each decision has involved the evaluation of a complex of factors, partly economic, partly political and partly concerned with the fundamentals of motor vehicle manufacture and sale. It has not always been possible to foresee the many shifts and changes in national policy, in the terms and movement of trade, or in the internal political affairs of nations.

Insofar as we did things well, it was the result, in large measure, of the fact that General Motors had a foundation of sound policies and a plan of operation that permitted us to make individual decisions promptly in the best interest of the business as a whole. It was also a result of the fact that General Motors people the world over have brought to the operation of the business a solid understanding of the General Motors approach, the technical know-how built out of long experience in the manufacture and distribution of motor vehicles and the skill to adapt to the particular operating conditions in countries overseas.

As is true in any successful business, the story of the people at all levels of the operation of the business is the key to understanding its performance.

4

THE PEOPLE WHO
MAKE IT POSSIBLE

CUSTOMERS, EMPLOYEES AND STOCKHOLDERS

The growth of General Motors as a world-wide industrial enterprise has depended upon its capacity to serve the varied and changing desires of people as customers both at home and abroad. This capacity to serve our customers, in turn, has depended upon people in two other roles—as employees and as owners of the business. It is people in these roles who have continued to provide the resources necessary to meet our ongoing challenges and opportunities. Correspondingly, these people must be given the incentives to work and to take the risks of ownership for the sustained growth and high performance of the enterprise.

The importance of people as employees of General Motors is evidenced by our personnel policies, many of which have been negotiated with labor unions, and by our continuing efforts directed toward the development of these policies. The interests of people as shareholders of General Motors are expressed in our policies, in our views toward ownership, and in the day-to-day efforts of our management to produce financial results that will speak well for themselves in the free investment markets of the world. The expansion of General Motors overseas has been made possible by the human and capital resources provided by our employees and shareholders. At the same time, this expansion has provided enlarged opportunity for present and potential employees and investors around the world.

WHAT A NEW OPERATION BRINGS TO A COUNTRY

The establishment of a manufacturing or assembly subsidiary in an overseas country provides a means for developing and employing local resources in accordance with the most advanced technology available to the world-wide enterprise. Additional employment opportunities for the citizens of each country are created by the infusion of capital and knowledge— modern machinery and equipment, and the latest marketing, manufacturing and management methods. To the extent that more and better tools and methods are provided, employees are given the opportunity to raise their productivity—the real basis for higher living standards.

Typically, the jobs created by the investments of a modern world-wide manufacturing concern demand higher skills than those generally required before. Along with the provision of tools and equipment must go an investment in the education and training of employees. In this way the technological results of years of experience, trial and error are provided in a matter of weeks or months. And the process is a continuing one. As still more efficient methods are developed, they are transmitted to all parts of the world through the multi-national enterprise.

Transference of management methods and technological skills overseas, even within the unified framework of a world-wide corporation, requires conscious and deliberate effort. Training and skill development must be based on an understanding of the people whose language, attitudes and social customs are often quite different from those of the home country, or from one region of the world to another. Employee training is an important part of building and maintaining a successful enterprise. Certainly this has been demonstrated in the examples of the American motor vehicle companies that have extended their operations overseas.

This necessity for investing in the education and training of the people to staff our operations overseas is most easily seen in a developing country where industrial activities are relatively new and limited to a small part of the national economy. On the other hand, though often taken for granted, training in the latest technology of practically every field of business and industry contributes importantly to the further progress of highly developed countries as well. Even in

79

an advanced nation such as the United States, there is much to be discovered and learned about industrial and economic progress. It seems clear that progress feeds on itself calling for an ever increasing amount of education and training effort. One of the major contributions of a world-wide enterprise is that its organization becomes a pipeline for the transmission of knowledge and progress wherever they appear in the world.

A new motor vehicle manufacturing or assembly operation brings to a country the advantage of new products or a wider range of consumer choice. And, if freely competitive market conditions are permitted to exist unencumbered by noneconomic trade restrictions, these products can be produced and sold at lower cost than would otherwise prevail. Once the operation gets under way, the foundation is laid for further improvement in the quality and value of the product with little or no addition to its cost. This permits an expansion of market volume which, in turn, stimulates the emergence and growth of a variety of related businesses serving the needs of motor vehicle owners and users. The employment and investment opportunities generated by the development of these businesses related to the use and enjoyment of the automobile are clearly evident in any nation where motor vehicle usage is an established fact.

Moreover, a motor vehicle manufacturing or assembly operation also provides direct stimulation to the development of local manufacturing industries which normally supply large quantities of specialized services, materials, parts and components to motor vehicle producers. Similarly, the expansion of dealer organizations for the marketing and servicing of motor vehicles provides a further contribution to the economic development of a country.

STAFFING OUR OPERATIONS AROUND THE WORLD

I am convinced that the capacity of a world-wide business to meet the challenges and opportunities provided by growing and changing world markets will continue to depend, above all, on the quality of its personnel. Soundly conceived principles of organization and competitive business strategy provide only the structure within which people can function creatively and productively. The degree of success achieved by a business enterprise depends, ultimately, on the ability, integrity, dedication and continuing personal satisfaction of its employees. A business organization is a meaningless concept apart from the people who staff it.

The human element has always been in the forefront of our thinking and planning in General Motors. A long-standing objective of our operating philosophy has been to provide a working environment which will encourage the development of the full skills and capabilities of our employees, and to endeavor to make each generation of management better than the one preceding it.

Seasoned and capable managerial manpower can be acquired by a business in only two ways. One is to hire people from the outside after they have gained training and experience in some other organization; the other is to train and promote employees within the company. Promotion from within has been, and continues to be, the focus of our policy in General Motors.

Our world-wide goal has been to recruit people with the capacity, desire and self-discipline for continuing growth, and to provide the training and working opportunities which will help them to attain higher managerial positions within the General Motors organization. There have been instances where a required skill or professional specialty was not available within the organization, and the only alternative was to hire a person from the outside. This practice, however, has been limited almost entirely to certain staff or professional positions, and it has been the exception rather than the rule. The career patterns and lengths of service of the senior management executives in General Motors testify to our emphasis on training and promotion from within the organization.

Turning more specifically to overseas personnel policy, we continually seek to provide a maximum of opportunity for the employment and advancement of the citizens of each country in which General Motors operates. This is reflected in the fact that out of our total overseas employment of close to 155,000 persons at the end of 1965, only 287 were assigned to overseas subsidiaries by the home office of our Overseas Operations Division. While most are United States citizens, there are some twenty who are citizens of other countries. All are executives with a high degree of technical or general management skill and experience in General Motors, not yet developed in individual overseas countries.

With rare exception, all of our overseas employees compensated on an hourly basis are citizens of the countries in which they are employed, or citizens of other overseas countries in instances where it has been national policy to supplement a nation's labor force with workers from other countries. In the case of our overseas salaried personnel, numbering more than 40,000 persons at the end of 1965, over 99 per cent have been recruited from countries abroad.

To the limited extent that employees from the United States have been assigned overseas, two considerations have been involved. First, there have been shortages of seasoned overseas personnel with a broad background of General Motors experience and a close understanding of the interdependence of our operations world-wide. Second, certain operating positions sometimes have required managerial or technical skills that, at the time, were unavailable overseas. Personnel from the United States have been assigned to such positions for periods only as long as they have been needed to assure that General Motors standards of technical know-how and commercial services would be maintained.

As our overseas personnel obtain the skill and experience required, I anticipate that the number of operating and staff specialists from the United States can be reduced even below present levels. This is a long-range objective, and we are making good progress toward its attainment. For example, when motor vehicle manufacturing was initiated in Australia, some 42 management and technical specialists from the United States were required. In early 1966, with an operation roughly ten times as large, Holden's employed only nine management people assigned from the United States.

To achieve the goal of employing local citizens, General Motors has developed, on a continuing basis, an intensive program of overseas manpower development through education and on-the-job training. From the fall of 1945 to 1966, General Motors scholarships were awarded to more than 500 overseas employees for two-year cooperative study programs at the General Motors Institute in Flint, Michigan. Of this postwar total, 412 overseas students graduated from the two-year programs, and 114 were enrolled in the spring of 1966. The scholarships have covered all the students' expenses for the courses of study in engineering offered by the General Motors Institute. These courses also have included periodic training assignments to our operating divisions in the United States.

In addition to the two-year overseas scholarship program, a substantial number of our overseas employees participate in other specialized training programs offered by the General Motors Institute. For example, from 1957 through 1965, a period covered by our comprehensive inventories of manpower training overseas, 207 overseas personnel have participated in other General Motors Institute programs.

Complementing the General Motors Institute programs are opportunities for in-service training in engineering, product development, manufacturing methods, marketing and finance. From 1957 through 1965, almost 1,000 employees came to the United States to participate in such programs, while an additional 1,000 employees received similar training in General Motors overseas facilities at locations other than their home bases.

General Motors also continues to emphasize formal

on-the-job training courses for overseas personnel within local facilities abroad. For example, in 1965, nearly 6,000 enrollments in apprenticeship and management training courses, and over 2,800 enrollments in nonmanagement courses, were recorded for overseas employees in various overseas locations.

The assignment of our employees to our other plants and offices around the world for training purposes is an integral part of the broad program of manpower development in General Motors. In 1965, about 400 short-term assignments of overseas personnel were made to the United States in all phases of our business for consultation and for updating and training in the latest methods. In total, these assignments covered nearly 12,000 man-days. Moreover, the flow of employees was not all one way. During 1965, employees from the United States also completed 400 assignments to overseas locations (for a total of 19,000 man-days) for training purposes and assisting in the application of improved methods. In my judgment, these coordinated and continuing efforts, focused on the solution of problems specifically related to the job, are among the most effective contributions General Motors is making in the area of manpower development overseas.

Programs which help our employees prepare for larger responsibilities are good business from our point of view. They help us to overcome the shortages of skilled manpower which are commonplace in many countries overseas. At the same time, they lay the foundation for an understanding of General Motors policy and of the role of the overseas subsidiary in the business as a whole. These are prerequisites for higher levels of management responsibility. Our corporate executives in this country must have a broad world-wide perspective, and we are striving to accomplish the same results overseas.

This breadth of view and understanding is essential to effective management overseas. In spite of the rapidity and ease of world travel and communications today, the manager of an overseas subsidiary must assume the responsibility for a wide range of decisions which demand a broad understanding of our business as a whole as well as a detailed knowledge of local conditions.

BECOMING A PART OF EACH COUNTRY

In this connection, I want to underscore the fact that a central objective of General Motors policy has always been to conduct its affairs in each country as a good citizen of that country. This goes well beyond strict conformity to the laws of the land. It includes respect for, and adherence to, the methods of conducting business and the commercial, social and cultural traditions of the country.

This policy rests on the fact that our primary reason

for participating in the economy of a nation is to perform those functions for which we are organized—to manufacture and sell motorized products and, in so doing, to use our resources productively and profitably. It is the responsibility of our management team overseas to accomplish this goal in a manner consistent with national policies and in the best interests of the business as a whole.

In practice, this has meant that our overseas managers and their staffs must understand and interpret changing local market conditions within the framework of the broader political and social trends in the environments in which they operate. When changes occur, economic or otherwise, our overseas managers bear the responsibility for estimating their impact on the established policies and practices of the enterprise, and if the changes are considered to be of strategic business importance, they are expected to submit new policy proposals to our governing committees. The basic criteria for evaluating such proposals are, first, to maintain an efficient and profitable overall business operation and, second, to identify each subsidiary as closely as possible with its country including provision for its maintenance and growth in relation to its earnings potential.

The nature of this dual objective can be illustrated by reference to a specific aspect of our policy—the compensation of hourly-rated and salaried employees. From a corporation-wide point of view, compensation policy is clearly established. In every country in which General Motors operates, the level of compensation must be consistent with local standards and fully competitive for the type of work performed and the skills required. This means that the level and form of compensation may vary from one country to another. In some countries, many elements in the compensation of employees are established by law, and there are great variations from country to country in terms of what is required. Tradition and custom may also play a part. In many nations overseas, the elements of compensation that are referred to in the United States as "fringe benefits" account for a much larger share of total compensation than in this country.

In General Motors, we have long recognized the importance of these national differences. We consider the adaptation of our compensation plans to these differences to be essential to the identification of each overseas subsidiary with its national economy. We reject the notion that a rigid compensation plan could be imposed on all of our subsidiaries overseas. Both the level of compensation and the form it assumes are properly matters to be decided, locally, between the plant manager and his employees within the context of national laws, practices and traditions.

This approach to managing our operations in each country recognizes a principle which, I believe, is valid world-wide. The success of any business enterprise is dependent on the economic health of its customers, and on the goodwill and cooperation of the government and the people of the country in which it operates. By identifying our business with the country, by adhering to its traditions and by sharing in its goals for growth, General Motors continually strives to achieve these requirements for success.

INCENTIVES FOR OUR EXECUTIVES OVERSEAS

To become a highly productive and fully integrated part of each national economy in which we locate, each subsidiary must also be closely coordinated and identified with overall General Motors operations and objectives. This is as essential for the effective business performance of the subsidiary as it is for the Corporation as a whole. Inclusion of all of our executive personnel in the General Motors incentive compensation plan has been a key element in identifying our individual overseas operations with the business as a whole.

An executive incentive compensation program has long been an important feature of our operations. Throughout the postwar period we have worked hard to extend the stock ownership aspect of this plan to our overseas subsidiaries, but it is only recently that this goal has been achieved.

The General Motors incentive compensation program for its executives is designed to stimulate and reward a high level of individual performance. Our overall level of salaries is expected to be competitive over a period of years with the salaries paid outside General Motors in the various countries in which we operate, and to be in line with the executive's level of responsibility and authority in the Corporation. The executive's incentive compensation, which adds to his salary, is related to three factors: the profitableness of the business as a whole, the contribution which the particular subsidiary or division has made to the business and the contribution of the individual.

A significant feature of the plan is that a large part of each bonus award is made in the form of General Motors common stock. This provides an essential link, in terms of the executive's compensation, between his interest as a part of management and his interest as an owner of the business. Bonus awards in the form of stock participation are extended to eligible executives on the basis of performance in all the countries where we operate except one. In that country, foreign exchange restrictions prevent an award of any part of the bonus in the form of General Motors stock.

A compensation plan which contributes to the identification of the executive with the overall performance of the business, as well as with his own part of the business, is an essential feature of the effective management of a world-wide business such as General Motors. Its value, however, extends beyond this. A plan of this type helps to familiarize citizens in many countries with stock ownership in general and, particularly, with stock ownership in an enterprise which is not limited in its operations to a single country.

For example, General Motors made stock awards for 1965 to nearly 850 executives outside the United States and Canada who were employed in twenty-one countries in which General Motors operates. I am personally very pleased with the progress of this program. In particular, I find it encouraging that executives outside the United States retain a large portion of the shares delivered to them, comparable to what they do in the United States.

OWNERSHIP POLICY: A CATALYST FOR GROWTH

Closely related to the General Motors incentive compensation plan is our policy of a unified ownership of overseas subsidiaries. Both follow logically from the inherent interdependence of our divisions and subsidiaries around the world. From an operational point of view, our overseas subsidiaries are as fully integrated in our overall operations as any division or plant in the United States. The fact that an overseas subsidiary is governed by the regulations of another sovereign nation does not alter this basic business relationship. Nor does the particular location of the operation in any way diminish the need for a coordinated approach to serving world markets. On the contrary, geographical dispersion makes the need for coordination even more compelling.

The strategic importance of a unified ownership of operating units was recognized at a very early stage in the development of General Motors overseas. A policy of coordinated control could be expected to result in improved business efficiency only if it had as its counterpart a policy of unified ownership. And as we have accumulated world-wide operating experience, our view on unified ownership has been strongly reinforced.

Full ownership of our overseas subsidiaries has permitted us to reach decisions involving these subsidiaries on the basis of sound business principles—on the same terms as our domestic divisions. This freedom to base our decisions on objective economic considerations has been valued so highly in General Motors that we have invested in new facilities, or maintained our investment in existing operations, only in those countries where national laws have been compatible with unified ownership. Where this has not been possible, we have tried to maintain an overseas market position through a network of franchised dealers who own their businesses, purchase our products on a regular commercial basis and distribute them locally. In some cases, these dealers perform certain assembly operations in order to minimize shipping costs and local import duties.

Unified ownership has made possible a continuous flow of technical assistance and know-how among General Motors divisions and subsidiaries throughout the world. This technical assistance has taken the form of new engineering developments, advanced manufacturing methods, improved machine design, more efficient production layouts and other requisites for creating high quality products at the lowest possible cost. At the same time, unified ownership has contributed to the efficiency of our distribution system—also helping to lower the costs of our products to the ultimate consumer—while the standards of our customer service have been extended and consistently maintained world-wide.

In emphasizing unified ownership of the business as essential to the efficiency of a company such as General Motors, it is important to underscore another fact. The growth of an overseas subsidiary enlarges the opportunity for employment and participation in the ownership of local businesses which supply materials and services to us, and of local dealerships which distribute and service our products.

A large share of the final sales price paid for General Motors products by the retail customer—on the average around 60 per cent in the overseas countries where we engage in motor vehicle manufacturing—is paid locally to supplying companies, wholesale distributors and retail dealerships, thereby expanding local business opportunity. Additional support is provided for the local development and ownership of many other businesses serving the needs of motor vehicle users throughout the country. Besides these expanded opportunities for local business ownership, an overseas operation brings direct benefit in the form of wages for the employees of the subsidiary and local taxes paid to the country where it operates. In short, by increasing the efficiency and market effectiveness of a world-wide enterprise like General Motors, unified ownership enlarges the opportunity for local participation in all businesses serving the production and use of motor vehicles, as well as the opportunity for employment and tax participation.

Of special interest, in countries such as England and West Germany, is the contribution which the manufacturing subsidiary has been able to make in expanding exports—a key factor in the economies of both countries. In 1965, for example, the combined exports of Opel and Vauxhall cars and trucks from these two countries amounted to about 447,000 units, or about 46 per cent of their total factory sales for the year. These exports were shipped throughout the world and had a wholesale value of over $560 million.

Behind these achievements is the fact that each General Motors subsidiary has full responsibility for developing its export markets world-wide. It is limited only by considerations of productive capacity, logistics, competition and tariff restrictions. The quality and attractiveness of Opel and Vauxhall vehicles have been important factors in their large export sales. But, of no less importance is the fact that these subsidiaries, being a part of General Motors, have had full access to our network of assembly and distribution facilities around the world. During the past ten years, about 43 per cent of the Opel and Vauxhall vehicles sold by the factory as exports have been shipped on an unassembled basis to General Motors assembly plants outside of Germany and England.

The overseas demand for Holden's vehicles produced in Australia has expanded more slowly, reflecting in part, the lower income levels in the export markets which Holden's can most advantageously serve. In 1965, exports, representing about 13 per cent of Holden's factory sales, were shipped to 61 different overseas territories. Although starting from a smaller base, Holden's export sales potential is being enlarged in the same way as the export potential of our other subsidiaries—by membership in the General Motors world-wide network of assembly and distribution facilities. Progress continues to be made in expanding Holden's exports. It may be noted that the foreign exchange generated by Holden's export sales in 1965 more than covered the exchange demands resulting from Holden's remission of dividends to the United States in that year. And I look forward to continuing gains in Holden's exports in the years ahead.

From my experience, I am firmly convinced that a unified ownership policy contributes to broad industrial and economic advance by increasing the efficiency and competitive effectiveness of the enterprise as a whole and of each individual operation. This conclusion is evident in the history of General Motors. It is one that I have been able to verify personally on numerous business trips to our overseas subsidiaries over a period of years. I have witnessed the growth of these subsidiaries, and I have talked to local suppliers whose businesses have expanded and prospered in step with this growth. I have visited the sales and service facilities of local dealers, and I have observed their expansion, both in number and in size.

Through many conversations with bankers, industrialists and government officials overseas, I have obtained an understanding of their strong desire to promote the growth of their national economies and their awareness of the potential of the multi-national enterprise in contributing to this objective. I have sensed their interest in obtaining the opportunity, for their fellow citizens and themselves, of greater participation in the world-wide enterprise.

In my view, one of our greatest challenges in the years ahead is to find ways to accomplish the objective of world-wide participation in the ownership of multi-national businesses.

A GOAL FOR THE WORLD-WIDE INDUSTRIAL ENTERPRISE

My thinking on this matter starts from a very simple fact. Most multi-national business enterprises are corporations. They are publicly owned with the privilege of ownership open to all who desire it through the purchase of stock. The corporate form of organization facilitates a broad base of ownership and, from the viewpoint of the business, the location or nationality of the shareholders presents no difficulty.

What we in General Motors would like to be able to do is to extend the opportunity for stock ownership participation to people overseas on the same basis as it is made available to people in the United States. If the situation around the world were as uncomplicated as it is for the Texas citizen who buys General Motors stock instead of trying to buy a share in the local assembly plant in Arlington, Texas, there would be no problem. But there are problems overseas—difficult but not insurmountable. Their solution requires some modification of existing laws—both in the United States and abroad—and new international agreements based upon negotiations with the countries affected.

In any country where we carry on assembly or manufacturing operations, we own assets that, hopefully over the years, will generate profits and yield dividends. A dividend payable by an overseas subsidiary is remitted in dollars to the United States parent company, and under present laws, the dividend is subject to income taxes. In addition, there is the possibility of dividend taxes and the risk of exchange restrictions. If a citizen of an overseas country wants to purchase stock in the parent company, he first may face exchange restrictions in buying the stock. Then, when dividends are paid to him by the parent company, he faces the further possibility of having to pay income and dividend taxes both in the United States and in his home country, as well as being subject to possible exchange regulations and restrictions.

The undesirability of this roundabout routing of

earnings and dividends is evident. The facts upon which a solution to the problem could be based are relatively simple. Earnings are being realized in the overseas country on General Motors operations there. A local citizen owning stock in General Motors—the parent company—is entitled to dividends on the parent company's stock. A simple approach would be for the overseas country to recognize dividend payments to the local holders of the parent's stock as being the equivalent, for tax purposes, of a payment of dividends by any locally-owned company to local stockholders. Such a direct application by the subsidiary of local funds for the payment of dividends on the parent's stock would also simplify foreign exchange problems.

What is thus required is a *de facto* routing of dividends to the overseas owner of the stock through the medium of the local subsidiary's earnings that are available for payment of dividends to the parent company. I recognize that this is difficult in practice requiring the negotiation of international trade conventions and tax treaties, possibly with accompanying implementing legislation. But the result, if successful, would do much to increase the free flow of investment funds among the free nations of the world.

If this could be accomplished, and the overseas country's tax rates on the ownership of stock in a

United States-based company like General Motors were no greater than the tax rates levied on the ownership of stock in a locally-based company, the choice of owning shares in either a local or a multi-national company like General Motors could be determined by sound investment considerations alone. Dividends could be paid overseas on the stock of the United States-based company with little or no international transfer of funds through the foreign exchange market.

If international restrictions on the purchase of stock could be reduced and if such a routing of dividends without local tax discrimination could be achieved, the same ownership opportunities we have in this country could be extended to the people of overseas countries where we carry on productive operations. There would be no conflict of ownership interests among the subsidiaries and, at the same time, the earnings realized in a given country would "stay at home" to the extent that dividends were paid by the parent company on stock acquired by the citizens of that country.

The importance of taking steps to encourage the international mobility of investment and earnings has received increasing recognition in recent years. For example, a study published in 1964 by the Presidential Task Force on Promoting Increased Foreign Investment in United States Corporate Securities, chairmanned by the present Secretary of the Treasury, Henry H. Fowler, focused on a number of recommendations for reducing impediments to the free flow of investment funds. These have, in part, been incorporated in a number of bills introduced in the Congress. They deserve most careful study.

With rising levels of personal income overseas, an increasing number of people can look forward to participating in business ownership through the purchase of corporate securities. Multi-national enterprise offers an attractive investment opportunity because its growth prospects are so clearly evident. Moreover, because it serves a large number of markets, investment in a world-wide corporation is less vulnerable to the normal business risks associated with exclusive dependence on a single market. This is a simple, but important, concept that should be explained and extended to people throughout the world.

STEPS TOWARD THE GOAL OF WORLD-WIDE OWNERSHIP

In addition to the discriminatory taxes and other obstacles to stock ownership in a world-wide enterprise which are within the authority of national governments, there are problems of a business character which those of us in business should recognize and help to resolve. Differences in accounting practices and financial reporting, differences in language and a lack of familiarity with companies based in other countries are also impediments to world-wide stock ownership.

With respect to standards of accounting and financial reporting, there are important differences among the countries of the world. It is to the great credit of our accounting profession, corporate management and the financial community as a whole, that sound principles of accounting have been generally accepted and widely adopted in the United States. I am encouraged by the progress being made in some countries abroad toward higher standards in these fields. While much remains to be accomplished, increasing recognition of the need for such standards and their adoption is coming in many other areas of the world. In the case of General Motors, I can assure you that we have consistently applied to all our overseas subsidiaries the same high standards of accounting which prevail in this country.

General Motors has taken a number of steps to attempt to overcome the obstacle of language and to raise the level of understanding of its operations worldwide. In addition to our full-length annual report published in this country and mailed to all stockholders at home and abroad, General Motors publishes condensed annual reports in German, French, Spanish and Portuguese for overseas distribution. In 1966, for example, summaries of our annual financial reports were placed in 30 leading newspapers and periodicals in Western Europe with a combined circulation of about 4.7 million. Our principal overseas manufacturing subsidiaries—Adam Opel in West Germany, Vauxhall in England and GM–Holden's in Australia—publish separate annual reports covering their operations.

The extension overseas of the listing of General Motors stock is another important part of our policy to promote world-wide ownership participation. The listing of a stock calls the attention of investors overseas to its availability and facilitates comparisons of prices and earnings. Today, General Motors stock is listed on most of the major stock exchanges of the world, including those in London, Frankfurt, Paris and Brussels, and it is traded in many other markets overseas organized for the purchase and sale of corporate securities.

The listing of General Motors stock on the London Stock Exchange is of special interest. This was undertaken in March of 1965 coincident with a secondary offering of about 2.8 million shares of General Motors common stock. Almost 500,000 shares (with a value of about $50 million) were sold overseas, with about 40 per cent being sold in the United Kingdom and the balance in other foreign countries. Of the total secondary offering in the United Kingdom, almost half (about 100,000 shares) was issued in the form of nearly two million Bearer Depositary Receipts Units with a "Unit" representing one-twentieth of a full share of General Motors common stock. These General Motors Depositary Receipts gave the small investor the opportunity of buying shares in a price range comparable to that at which the shares of other companies were traded in the United Kingdom. They were the first such receipts representing the shares of an American company to be listed on the London Stock Exchange.

Partly as a result of these efforts, the number of shares of General Motors common stock held outside the United States has increased substantially. The extent of this increase in General Motors stock ownership cannot be judged accurately, because many shares owned by investors outside the United States are held in the names of nominees. Insofar as holdings could be identified, they amounted to about 6.5 million shares in 1965. Altogether, General Motors stockholders represented more than 80 countries of the world.

Our desire to broaden our base of ownership is consistent with General Motors world-wide business approach, as well as being aimed directly at our larger objective to help raise the level of economic opportunity wherever we operate in the world. What we have achieved so far, of course, is only a beginning. I hope that our efforts may continue to bear fruit in the form of a growing base of ownership until the citizens of all of the nations and markets of the world which General Motors serves are fully represented.

My deep convictions on the matter of unified ownership derive from the unusual privilege I have had for an observation of world business at first hand. I have seen what can be accomplished by an ownership concept which facilitates unity, coordinated policy determination and sound operating procedures.

5

CONCLUSION

Let me summarize our overseas record during the past fifteen years in terms of some objective measures of business accomplishment. At the end of 1950, the value of General Motors net working capital and fixed assets overseas was about $180 million. This investment represented a fair estimate of General Motors stake in world markets as the postwar rebuilding process began to gain momentum. By the close of 1965, this investment had increased to about $1.1 billion, or approximately six times the amount in 1950.

This expansion was accomplished almost entirely from financial resources generated through General Motors operations overseas and through local borrowings which would be repaid out of local earnings. As a result, the expansion of each overseas subsidiary has been geared to the volume of its business and its resources, consistent with yielding a competitive return to the owners of the business. General Motors subsidiaries have distributed through dividend remittances to the parent corporation all earnings that were not required to meet the demands on the business overseas. During the postwar years, our overseas subsidiaries remitted about two-thirds of their earnings to the United States. This is close to the percentage of General Motors Corporation earnings distributed in the form of dividends.

In 1950, total production of General Motors overseas manufacturing subsidiaries was about 180,000 cars and trucks. By 1965, this total had increased to about 1.2 million units. Production by Opel in West Germany, which was nonexistent in the postwar years prior to 1948, totaled more than 635,000 units in 1965—a volume which came close to matching the production of Oldsmobile or Buick in the United States. And the General Motors facility at Russelsheim in West Germany—only a part of our Opel manufacturing operation—had become the largest single manufacturing facility on one site in the entire General Motors Corporation.

Taking into account General Motors world-wide facilities, including those in the United States and Canada, factory sales increased from 4 million vehicles in 1950 to 7.3 million in 1965. About 30 per cent of this increase—almost 1 million units—was a result of the growth in our overseas manufacturing operations. Our overseas operations serve their domestic markets and, in addition, export to markets in all areas of the world where there is a demand for their vehicles. Over this same period, the combined exports of all of our overseas manufacturing subsidiaries, more than 3.9 million cars and trucks, have represented over 40 per cent of these subsidiaries' combined sales.

General Motors must measure these world-wide accomplishments both in terms of a freedom of investment and a freedom of trade. Our domestic and overseas operations compete with each other. But, it does not follow that as our manufacturing operations are enlarged overseas, our potential for exporting from the United States is reduced accordingly. On the contrary, our experience shows that our investments overseas have improved our ability to export, sell and service our products made in the United States.

The type and location of our overseas investments are dictated by market considerations, including the capacity to compete for export markets. By reducing unit costs to the consumer, these investments promote an expansion of export sales. I am convinced that General Motors car and truck exports from the United States, and from other countries abroad, have been supported and facilitated by our world-wide assembly and distribution facilities.

Here we come to the heart of the matter. General Motors accomplishments derive from two simple axioms of competitive free enterprise. First, the business must design, manufacture and distribute products that its customers want to buy. Second, it must organ-

111

ize, invest and manage itself so as to serve these customers efficiently and use its resources profitably. These are our primary objectives.

To the extent that General Motors has succeeded in attaining these goals, its world-wide operations have provided other benefits as well. General Motors, along with similar multi-national businesses, has made the products of modern science and technology available in greater abundance and at lower cost than was ever possible before. Motor vehicles which incorporate the most advanced developments in many branches of science and technology are today making contributions in areas of the world where an understanding of this technology is limited. Viewed in terms of the long and costly history of invention and innovation, the result is to hurdle barriers of time and cost, making it possible for developing countries to enjoy the benefits of man's achievements in his relentless search for a better life through industrial progress.

With the growth of General Motors and other motor vehicle producers, world-wide competition has intensified. It is difficult to find areas of the world today which are not served by two or more motor vehicle producers competing vigorously and seeking to expand their positions in the market. This competitive rivalry in the quest for markets and profits is the best assurance that customers, wherever they may live, will be served with products of the type and quality they want at the lowest possible cost.

In this record of accomplishment lies the promise of world-wide industrial concerns. In the long history of world economic progress they represent a new force for growth—keenly competitive in all aspects, aggressive in a search for the markets they can best serve, sensitively flexible in their adjustment to change, and creative through innovation inspired by the hope of profit.

The world-wide industrial enterprise is a powerful force for economic growth which transcends national boundaries but respects national goals. It strives to serve a variety of diverse markets efficiently. In being an active and an adaptive participant in the industrial growth of the world, it seeks to advance the economic interests of every country in which it participates.

The world-wide enterprise is a force that can be used to bring the advanced technology of products, materials, methods and processes quickly and efficiently to the service of nations throughout the world; it can impart new labor skills to populations; and it can provide the best in marketing techniques and in management methods and talent.

In short, the world-wide enterprise is potentially a most effective element in a world-wide desire for economic growth. Used well in an environment of freedom, it offers a potential unlimited today and in the years ahead. It provides an important element in the search for world peace. These are the objectives which constitute the ultimate challenge and the promise of world-wide industrial enterprise.

Appendix

ORGANIZATIONAL AND STATISTICAL CHARTS

CHART 1

ORGANIZATION CHART

GENERAL MOTORS CORPORATION

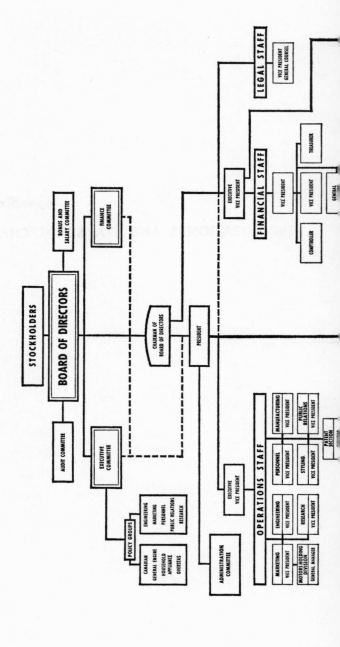

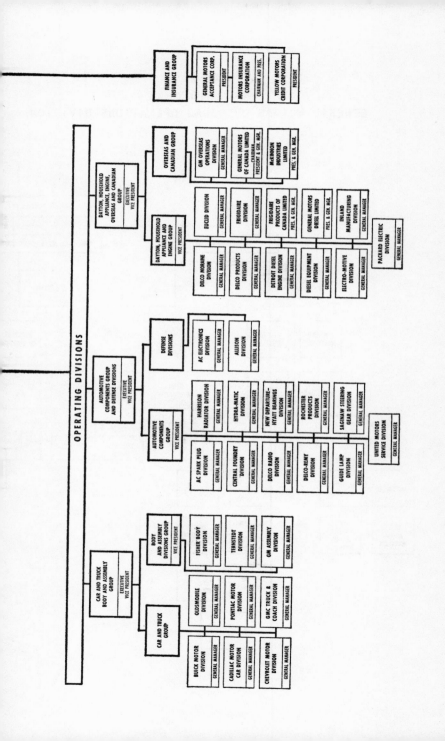

CHART 2

ORGANIZATION CHART

GENERAL MOTORS OVERSEAS OPERATIONS DIVISION

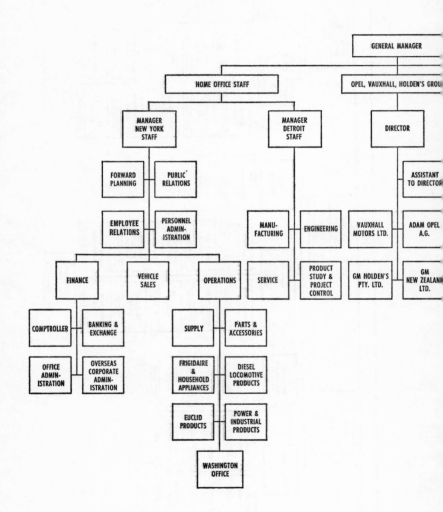

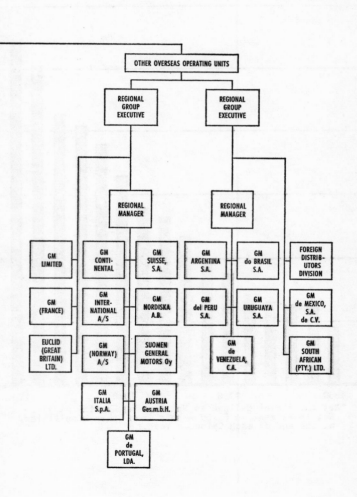

OTHER OVERSEAS OPERATING UNITS

REGIONAL GROUP EXECUTIVE

REGIONAL GROUP EXECUTIVE

REGIONAL MANAGER

REGIONAL MANAGER

GM LIMITED

GM CONTI-NENTAL

GM SUISSE, S.A.

GM ARGENTINA S.A.

GM do BRASIL S.A.

FOREIGN DISTRIB-UTORS DIVISION

GM (FRANCE)

GM INTER-NATIONAL A/S

GM NORDISKA A.B.

GM del PERU S.A.

GM URUGUAYA S.A.

GM de MEXICO, S.A. de C.V.

EUCLID (GREAT BRITAIN) LTD.

GM (NORWAY) A/S

SUOMEN GENERAL MOTORS Oy

GM de VENEZUELA, C.A.

GM SOUTH AFRICAN (PTY.) LTD.

GM ITALIA S.p.A.

GM AUSTRIA Ges.m.b.H.

GM de PORTUGAL, LDA.

CHART 3

GENERAL MOTORS NET INVESTMENT*
OUTSIDE THE UNITED STATES AND CANADA, 1950 - 65

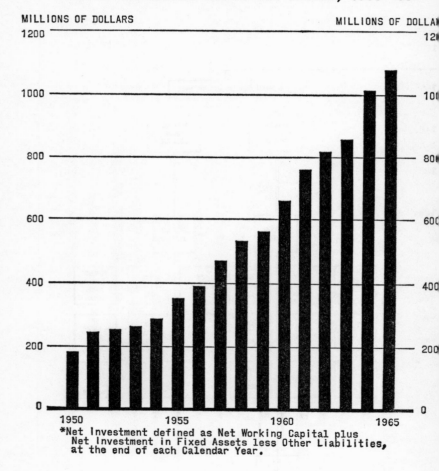

MILLIONS OF DOLLARS

MILLIONS OF DOLLARS

*Net Investment defined as Net Working Capital plus
 Net Investment in Fixed Assets less Other Liabilities,
 at the end of each Calendar Year.

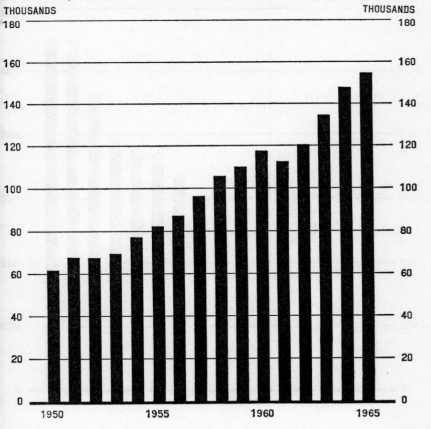

CHART 4

GENERAL MOTORS EMPLOYMENT
OUTSIDE THE UNITED STATES AND CANADA, 1950-65
Average Number of Hourly and Salaried Employees

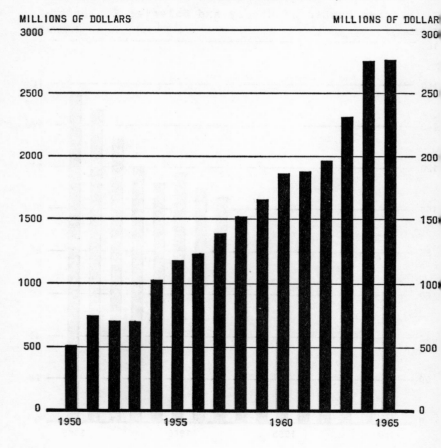

CHART 5

GENERAL MOTORS NET SALES
OUTSIDE THE UNITED STATES AND CANADA, 1950 - 65

CHART 6

GENERAL MOTORS OVERSEAS MANUFACTURING SUBSIDIARIES' CAR AND TRUCK FACTORY SALES, DOMESTIC AND EXPORT, 1950 - 65

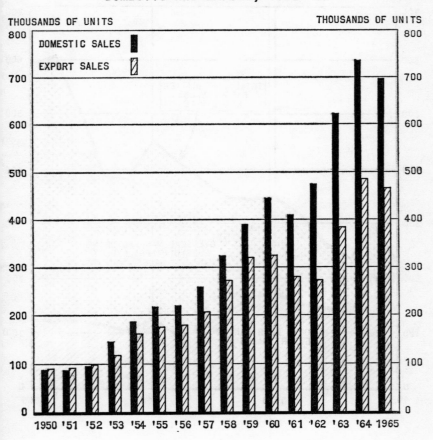

CHART 7

GENERAL MOTORS
CAR AND TRUCK EXPORT SALES WORLD-WIDE, 1950 - 65

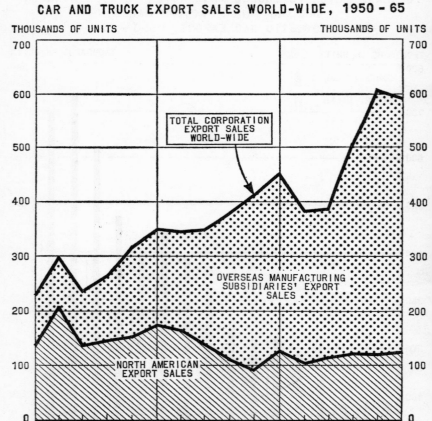